LUCINDA COXON

Lucinda Coxon's work has been produced at The Bush Theatre, Soho Theatre and the National Theatre in London, and at South Coast Repertory, the Magic Theatre and the Ohio Theatre Space NY in the US. Her plays include *Waiting at the Water's Edge*, *Wishbones*, *Three Graces*, *The Ice Palace*, *Nostalgia*, *Vesuvius* and a translation of Lorca's *The Shoemaker's Incredible Wife*. Her film work includes *Spaghetti Slow* and *The Heart of Me*.

Lucinda Coxon

HAPPY NOW?

NICK HERN BOOKS

London

www.nickhernbooks.co.uk

A Nick Hern Book

Happy Now? first published in Great Britain in 2008 as a paperback original by Nick Hern Books Limited, 14 Larden Road, London W3 7ST

Happy Now? copyright © 2008 Lucinda Coxon

Lucinda Coxon has asserted her right to be identified as the author of this work

Cover design: www.energydesignstudio.com

Typeset by Nick Hern Books, London
Printed and bound in Great Britain by CPI Antony Rowe

A CIP catalogue record for this book is available from the British Library

ISBN 978 1 85459 560 7

Happy Now? was first performed in the Cottesloe auditorium of the National Theatre, London, on 24 January 2008 (previews from 16 January), with the following cast:

MICHAEL	Stanley Townsend
KITTY	Olivia Williams
JOHNNY	Jonathan Cullen
MILES	Dominic Rowan
BEA	Emily Joyce
CARL	Stuart McQuarrie
JUNE	Anne Reid

Director   Thea Sharrock
Designer   Jonathan Fensom
Lighting Designer   Oliver Fenwick
Sound Designer   Paul Arditti

HAPPY NOW?

Lucinda Coxon

To Bretia, Tom and Lily

Characters

KITTY
MICHAEL
JOHNNY, *Kitty's husband*
MILES
BEA, *Miles' wife*
CARL
JUNE, *Kitty's mother*

All characters are in their late thirties except for Michael who is late forties, and June who is in her sixties.

Unlike the others, Michael and June have retained slight (different) regional accents.

The place is the city, the time is now.

It was my original intention – and it would still be perfectly possible – for the actor playing Michael also to play June, Kitty's mother. In this case, the actor should wear the clothes of a portly woman in late middle age and a neat grey wig. He should remain, unmistakably, a man in perfunctory drag.

L.C.

This text went to press before the end of rehearsals and so may differ slightly from the play as performed.

ACT ONE

Scene One

Hotel bar, the aftermath of a conference. Muzak plays. Voices rise and fall. A man, MICHAEL, holds court. He's colourful, expansive, slightly loosened up with drink and tiredness. He tells a joke to a group of (unseen) male colleagues.

MICHAEL. So afterwards, he says to her, the guy says . . . 'If I'd known you were a virgin I'd've taken more time . . . ' and she says . . . she says . . .

He laughs in anticipation of his punchline . . .

'If I'd known you had more time, I'd have taken my tights off!'

Uproarious reaction . . . MICHAEL does a little victory dance, in the midst of which he sees KITTY walk through the bar. He's instantly struck by her.

Sorry – *mea culpa* – ladies present . . .

KITTY. No problem.

She keeps moving, but MICHAEL delays her, engaging with her directly.

MICHAEL. Still, I always think the average woman can take a joke. You know what the proof of that is?

KITTY *smiles a little, not especially out of pleasure.*

KITTY. No.

MICHAEL. The average man.

KITTY *manages to raise her eyebrows in acknowledgement of the attempt, but doesn't laugh.*

Oh – I'm dying here. God, somebody shoot me, put me out of my misery.

KITTY. Don't worry about it.

MICHAEL. It's you. You make me nervous.

KITTY (*sarcastic*). Really?

She stiffens, goes to leave.

MICHAEL. Sorry – Michael. Michael Manson.

He displays his conference badge.

Age Awareness.

KITTY*'s attitude shifts.*

KITTY. Oh, I've heard of you . . . er, Kitty Allison, Cancer . . .

MICHAEL. Cancer Concern – I know – I saw you up there.

He puffs out his cheeks, a pantomime of amazement.

I mean, your presentation – blew me away . . . I tell you, I was like – you go, girl.

KITTY (*uncertainly*). Thank you.

MICHAEL. It needed saying what you were saying – and no one ever says it.

KITTY *relaxes a little, on professional ground.*

KITTY. Well it's unpalatable.

MICHAEL. But it's the truth! What are we going to do – carry on for ever living in this . . . this threadbare fantasy that someday our prince of core funding will come? No – that's gone. He's over the hills and far away. Organisations like ours have to *embrace* that. Say: okay, maybe we haven't got the stability the one big government grant would give us, but what we have got is flexibility – a crack at self-determination. I'm very excited. I'm sorry. You excited me.

KITTY *gestures a politely ambivalent response.*

Will you have a drink?

She's tempted, but:

KITTY. You know what, I won't, thanks.

MICHAEL. No, quite right. Stay in control. Not like this rabble.

He gestures to the men.

Like kids on a school outing. Me too. I'll put my hand up.

KITTY. It's just I've some stuff to write up and then an early train home tomorrow . . .

MICHAEL. Sure. But sit, will you . . . two minutes. I'd love just to talk to you . . .

KITTY *hesitates a moment, then . . . she exhales, conscious suddenly of being tired.*

KITTY. Well why not?

She sits.

MICHAEL. It takes it out of you.

KITTY. It's just – you know – the adrenalin crash. I was more nervous than I expected to be.

MICHAEL. Didn't show.

KITTY. Bigger crowd than I'm used to. My boss usually does these events . . .

MICHAEL. Stephanie.

KITTY. Yes . . .

MICHAEL. I know Steph. We're on a government euthanasia panel together. I'm for. She's against.

KITTY. Oh . . . that's company policy. Anyway, she's got this throat thing they can't seem to knock out, so I stepped in. A bit seat-of-the-pants, to be honest.

MICHAEL. Come on! You did a terrific job. Cut yourself a bit of slack there.

KITTY. Yeah. Maybe.

MICHAEL. Have that drink.

KITTY. No . . . I might get a glass on the way up to my room, but . . .

MICHAEL. You've still work to pull in, then an early train.

KITTY. That's right.

MICHAEL. Then home.

KITTY. Yes.

MICHAEL. Kids?

KITTY. Two.

MICHAEL. Never stops, does it?

KITTY. No.

MICHAEL. Even with one. How old?

KITTY. Five and seven.

MICHAEL. That's a great age. But hard work. Thirteen now, my boy.

KITTY. Ah. A teenager.

MICHAEL. Yeah, a good one. We've been very lucky. Well – it's not all luck, is it . . . ? I mean, my wife's amazing with him. More patience than me. I'm alright for keeping things interesting but that's no good without someone doing the real work, you know. No, I'm like ice cream or something. Okay for a treat but you need to eat your vegetables.

Not that my wife's a vegetable.

KITTY. No.

She laughs in spite of herself.

MICHAEL. Planning more . . . ?

(*He clarifies.*) . . . Kids.

KITTY. Oh – no . . . I don't think so.

MICHAEL. Undecided.

KITTY. No – I'm sure. It's . . .

MICHAEL. It's enough.

KITTY. Exactly.

MICHAEL. Time for you now.

KITTY. Look, I think I read a paper you wrote: 'Charity Marketing in a New Millennium.'

MICHAEL. Guilty as charged.

KITTY. It was a *very* good piece: really thought through . . . And – God! – original. I've quoted from it.

MICHAEL. I'm delighted.

He leans forward, places his hand on KITTY*'s leg – a firm, unembarrassed gesture.*

Oh Kitty. You excited me.

KITTY *looks at his hand, moving up and down her leg now. She's astonished.*

KITTY. What's this?

MICHAEL. What?

KITTY. *This.*

He looks down at the hand.

MICHAEL. That? That's nothing.

KITTY. So let's stop it.

MICHAEL. Really?

KITTY *pushes his hand off angrily, looks around embarrassed.*

I'm sorry – I've made you uncomfortable.

KITTY. No, you've pissed me off. I'm going.

MICHAEL. Hey, don't . . . Look, I am sorry . . . That was horribly misjudged, I've made an idiot of myself . . . But please . . . Please . . . ?

He touches her arm, manages to get her back in the chair . . .
Then:

You're not really pissed off.

KITTY. I am really pissed off.

MICHAEL. I don't think this is how you are when you're
pissed off.

KITTY. I don't think you know me well enough to make that
judgement.

MICHAEL. Well I would like to.

He gestures – an open palm. KITTY *holds up her ring finger.*

KITTY. I'm married.

MICHAEL. I'm not suggesting bigamy.

KITTY. Tsk.

MICHAEL. Look, I just don't think it's the end of the world for
people to take pleasure in one another. Men and women in
peace and harmony in mid-price hotel chains all over the
world. If that's not for you – fine.

KITTY. It's not.

MICHAEL. Perfect. We're good.

KITTY *absorbs his apparent surrender.*

KITTY. So you do this a lot?

He gestures between himself and KITTY.

MICHAEL. This . . . ? Yes I do. Yes I do.

KITTY. Your poor wife.

MICHAEL *smiles.*

MICHAEL. You don't have to worry about my wife. My
family's the most precious thing under the sun to me. I take
very good care of them.

KITTY. Really.

MICHAEL. Don't be petty. Doesn't suit you.

KITTY. Ha!

MICHAEL. You're beautiful.

KITTY. Stop that.

MICHAEL. It's true.

KITTY. No, it's not . . .

MICHAEL. I think you're beautiful.

KITTY. Am I meant to be grateful?

MICHAEL. God, no. I'm the grateful one. You're supposed to be . . . apprised of the facts. That's all. Are you sure you won't have a drink. Just some water, or Coke or whatever . . . ?

KITTY. No thanks.

MICHAEL. Do you mind if I . . .

He gestures for a refill.

I find towards the end of the day, I'm glad to take the edge off things.

He settles back. She takes him in.

You've gone quiet.

Cat got your tongue, Kitty?

She flashes a warning look. MICHAEL *regroups.*

Kitty your real name?

KITTY. Yes.

MICHAEL. Not short for anything? Katherine? Kathleen?

KITTY. No, just Kitty.

MICHAEL. Y'get teased at school?

KITTY. The odd meow.

MICHAEL. Did they call you Pussy, Kitty?

KITTY. Right, that's it.

MICHAEL. Oh come on, it's a joke. I'm a clown.

KITTY. No – you're not.

MICHAEL. I'm a harmless fool.

KITTY. No, you're a tiresome opportunist who tells clever women they're beautiful and beautiful women they're clever and hopes they're too tired or pissed or lonely to tell the difference.

MICHAEL laughs, recklessly confident.

MICHAEL. So that's me! I make passes at women. What a crime!

He warms to his theme.

I make women laugh in spite of themselves. Stupid jokes so they're never threatened by my rapier wit! And once they've relaxed a bit, guess what . . . ? Yes – I make a move on them . . . Just casually, socially first off . . . no pressure there . . . but if they get comfortable with the occasional glancing whatever, then . . . yes . . .

KITTY. What . . . ?

MICHAEL. I kiss them! Women like that, they like to be kissed! Their husbands don't kiss them any more – why is that . . . ? Why don't men kiss their wives . . . ? Oh I love the face you're making there – 'My husband kisses me' – but he doesn't. You see women are so loyal, they're amazing – I think my wife would do the same as you, but it's not true. I don't kiss her. I kiss other women.

He savours his own predicament.

I kiss other women and it's delicious.

And if I were a better-looking man I'd maybe get my face slapped at that point but I'm this out-of-shape clown, so they're more surprised than anything else. And if I get turned down, well that's no problem, I'm not going to get nasty, I've no vanity. But if it goes okay – great. I make love to them. What exactly's so bad about that?

KITTY. 'Make love'?

MICHAEL. Yeah, make love, fuck, whatever they want to call it.

KITTY. What do *you* want to call it?

MICHAEL. Whatever's appropriate to call it in the circumstances, depending on how things've developed.

KITTY. Oh – so at this point the women are granted some individuation. This one bangs, that one screws . . . ?

MICHAEL. You know I would never use language like that and I expect better of you . . . What are you so angry about? Okay, so you think I'm indiscriminate. Well you know that is true up to a point. It's true in that I love women, and I don't discriminate between them on superficial grounds. Asian, black and pink women. Skinny – great, big ones – great. Slightly uptight – God-knows-with-good-reason – over-achieving athletic types like you – great. I'm not a tit man or a leg man – I'm a woman man. I'm a great leveller, Kitty. I make you all the same. You'd be surprised how many women find that a relief.

KITTY (*aghast*). Dear God, does this actually work sometimes?

MICHAEL. Always! It works always –

KITTY *laughs*.

KITTY. Yeah, right.

MICHAEL (*serious now*). Oh Kitty, make no mistake.

He catches her hand to secure her attention. She pulls away slightly but he holds on . . . He's utterly sincere now . . .

It is foolproof. Look – I make an offer . . . I've made you an offer. And you – you can take me up on the offer or you can turn me down. But the offer remains on the table. And we're bound by that. Even if you walk away. And at night when you're turning this over in your head, thinking what a prick I am, and yet how I took it so well when you knocked me back, there comes a niggling little bit of you that wonders why I didn't put up more of a fight about it.

And your mind begins to whirr . . .

KITTY *pulls her hand free, but is unable to stop listening.*

. . . and then, one day, something goes wrong for you, some small thing but with the life you're trying to lead – pulled in so many different directions – it's just the kind of thing that breaks the camel's back. And you just want to feel better about yourself, and you try some very expensive chocolate, and you try a glass of really good red wine and then you start to wonder . . . you start to think: I wonder if that sadsack guy still wants to be nice to me.

And the fact is, I do.

KITTY *is horribly mesmerised now.* MICHAEL *presses on, solicitous, insistent . . .*

And you'll come to me – we'll meet just for a drink after work on some trumped-up professional pretext, or you'll contrive to run into me at some other conference down the line . . . and you'll find yourself in a good place, then, Kitty. A safe place where no one will judge you for lowering your standards just far enough to get what you really want. Really need.

And even though you're a clever, beautiful woman – because that's true with you – you're both – even though you're a woman of the world and you're wise to its deceptions, this will happen to you. You think it won't – you think now I've told you how the trick works you just couldn't fall for it, right?

But you will, cos the trick is, there's no trick.

The sex is on the table. And the truth is, Kitty, that one day that's right where you'll want it.

KITTY *is stunned. The deafening sound of a train hurtling along, the flashing of light as it speeds through the landscape.* KITTY *braces against it.* MICHAEL *goes off.* KITTY *hurries to get out her phone. The sound stops.*

We continue straight into:

Scene Two

KITTY*'s kitchen.* KITTY *talks into the phone as she takes off her jacket, rearranges the space, transforms it into her home.*

KITTY. I mean, honestly . . . I know, I know . . . he actually said that . . . this out-of-shape clown of a guy.

Unbelievable.

Course it hasn't worked, how has it worked?

I'm talking about him because I'm annoyed, not intrigued. And if I can't talk to *you* . . . I mean, what's the use of a gay best friend if you can't . . .

Well thanks, Carl . . .

Listen, I need to get on, I have to get the kids' dinner . . .

No, I just got in, just a minute ago.

No, he's working late. Parents' interviews. It's his first time, I think he's quite nervous.

Oh, the usual – half a gallon of milk swilling around in the bottom of the fridge where some idiot's opened the carton and laid it on its side. I tell you, if I ever left for more than a day they'd go feral. Hey . . . how are you by the way? – I should've asked sooner, you sound a bit . . .

She pulls a face.

Oh, yeuch! Cos I thought you sounded weird before . . .

Well don't put Blistex inside cos it really stings. It'll heal on its own, it's a nice warm damp place.

A door slams offstage.

Oh shit, the kids just got dropped off . . .

BOY'S VOICE. Hi . . .

KITTY (*calling*). Hi!

GIRL'S VOICE. Hi . . .

KITTY (*calling*). Hi, hi . . . d'you miss me . . . ?

No answer. She goes back to the phone.

Listen: you need to tell that new himbo of yours there's a difference between a blowjob and face-fucking. Okay?

She laughs, shaking off the burden of the previous scene.

Hey, you cheered me up. Gotta get into mom mode. Bye bye.

KITTY *hangs up the phone. The theme tune of a kid's TV show plays.*

(*Calls.*) Are you not coming through . . . ?

No reply. KITTY walks towards the TV sound. She looks off-stage at her children for a moment, smiles. But she doesn't go to them.

KITTY *comes back, sets up two plastic cups on a table. Two plates. She looks at the table for a while, oddly pensive. A different theme tune kicks in.*

BOY'S VOICE. Mum, what's for tea . . . ?

KITTY *rallies a little.*

KITTY. Hmm . . . ? Oh – sandwiches . . .

She opens her briefcase . . .

BOY'S VOICE. Can we have them watching TV . . . ?

KITTY *looks at the just-set table, considers.*

GIRL'S VOICE. Please please! Daddy let us!

Whatever.

KITTY. Okay, just this once.

She takes two packets from the briefcase, reads . . .

There's tuna mayonnaise and BLT.

KITTY *still seems distracted. She throws the packets off-stage, towards the children's voices. She looks back to the briefcase.*

And fruit for after.

She rolls two apples offstage after the sandwiches, closes the briefcase.

She settles into the chair. Another kid's TV theme rolls over her.

Then another, and another.

Then the TV sound stops. The silence is striking. It is darker now. KITTY *hasn't noticed.*

GIRL'S VOICE. Are you going to read bedtime stories?

KITTY sits up surprised, disorientated, as though woken from a deep sleep.

KITTY. Er . . . sure, I'll be up in just a moment. Put the story tape on while you're waiting . . .

Silence for a moment, then a man's charming, sing-song voice begins . . . it is MICHAEL'*s voice.*

MICHAEL'S VOICE. Long, long ago in a far away place –

KITTY leans back in the chair, listens . . .

– lived a kind king and queen who had everything they wished for, except for the thing they wanted the most.

A man enters – JOHNNY *– he looks tired.* KITTY *looks up at him.*

JOHNNY. God, I'm sorry I'm late. I'm so late. Every appoint-ment overran . . .

He lays his hand on KITTY'*s head as he passes. Takes off his jacket. Rubs his face.*

Are *you* okay? How was it?

But KITTY *just looks at him, hostile, suspicious.*

What . . . ? What's the matter?

Beat.

Kitty . . . ? What is it . . . ?

KITTY. Why don't you kiss me any more?

Blackout.

Transition: a hospital monitor is projected on the back wall. The steady beep beep beep of someone sleeping, in recovery. Then a phone begins to ring. It rings and rings and rings until:

Scene Three

KITTY*'s, evening. The doorbell rings.* KITTY *struggles to get into a clean shirt.*

KITTY. Shit.

(*Shouts.*) Johnny . . . ?

JOHNNY *appears.*

I'm not ready . . . I haven't had time to get changed. Cora made me read *Sleeping Beauty* seven times before she'd go down.

JOHNNY. You look great.

KITTY. No I don't.

JOHNNY. They're our friends.

KITTY. They're your friends.

He holds her, no trace of their last encounter.

JOHNNY. You look fine.

KITTY. They'll look better.

JOHNNY. Impossible.

He's breaking away when . . .

KITTY. Hey Johnny – I'm thinking I might join a gym.

JOHNNY. What?

KITTY. If I find one that opens early enough.

JOHNNY. Are you joking?

KITTY. It's not a big thing but at the hospital when I was visiting Dad, they said I should get tested for type 2 diabetes, cos it runs in families and I might be prediabetic. So I went to see Dr Cunningham . . .

JOHNNY. You got tested . . . ?

KITTY. No – but I asked her what would happen if I *did* and turned out to be prediabetic. And she said then, lifestyle changes were a big thing, and studies showed if you exercised two hours a week and lost five per cent of your body weight you could stave off ever . . .

JOHNNY. So you didn't get tested?

KITTY. No.

JOHNNY. Why not?

KITTY. I don't want to be ill.

JOHNNY. It wouldn't mean you were ill . . .

KITTY. I don't want to be like him.

JOHNNY. Right.

The doorbell again, insistent this time.

KITTY. Go . . .

   JOHNNY *hesitates.*

   Go. Go – go on. It's not a big thing! Really . . .

   KITTY *hurries off.* JOHNNY *has a moment alone, then* MILES *walks into the scene with him. Opens his arms. They greet each other warmly.*

JOHNNY. Miles, you look terrific.

MILES. Took the kids sailing last weekend. Seem t've caught what there was of the sun.

JOHNNY. Catch anything else?

MILES. Sorry?

JOHNNY. Fish?

MILES. Sailing, Johnny. Sailing, not fishing.

JOHNNY. Not the same?

MILES. Stop being a twit.

JOHNNY. I'm just not conversant with . . .

MILES. Taking the piss.

JOHNNY *smiles, rumbled.*

JOHNNY. Red or white? Or there's beer in the fridge.

MILES *deliberates a second.*

MILES. White. White to start with.

JOHNNY *pours.*

Red on white, you'll be alright. White on red, better off dead.

JOHNNY. Cheers. What's happened to the girls . . . ?

MILES. Oh – Bea's showing Kitty the architects' plans.

MILES *grimaces.*

JOHNNY. Bored already? You've hardly got started . . .

MILES. Well it's her thing really. I just cough up the cash and try and look interested.

JOHNNY. Yeah, right.

MILES. Oh, every now and then she gives me a choice about something – you know, 'Do you think beige, cream, blossom, taupe, ecru, eau-de-Nil or stone, Miles?' and I have a go – you know – mull it over . . . and 'Stone,' I'll say. Then she does the mouth thing, and gets all . . .

He 'does' his wife, shaking her head in bewilderment.

And I say: 'What . . . ?' And she goes . . .

KITTY *and* BEA *appear – in a separate scene.* BEA *carries a rolled-up blueprint.*

BEA *and* MILES (*disproportionately hurt*). Don't you think 'stone's' a bit *cold*?

BEA. And he got so angry, he said:

BEA *and* MILES (*incredibly angry now*). 'Why d'you bloody ask if you just want to make the decision yourself? I mean, why ask the question if you already know the answer?'

KITTY and JOHNNY recoil, shocked. MILES shakes off the remembered anger, laughs – not entirely convincingly. The men drink. Our focus is on the women now.

BEA. It's a good thing though, in the end.

She looks to KITTY *for confirmation.* KITTY *nods, not altogether persuaded.*

I mean, you just reach that stage, don't you, where you need a joint project. You see other people's marriages going off the rails. And you think: we need a joint project.

KITTY *laughs, trying to leaven things.*

KITTY. Aren't the kids a joint project?

BEA. You need something outside of that. Something to help you reassess your core relationship, move forward together as a couple.

KITTY. So that's why you're glassing in the side return?

BEA. It's not just the side return. There'll be a new downstairs loo as well.

KITTY *nods to the plans.*

KITTY. It looks great.

The doorbell. KITTY *looks round, happy, relieved . . .*

Carl.

CARL *enters the scene with the men.* JOHNNY *takes his coat. The women pack up the plans . . .*

MILES. Carl – so, no Antoniou?

CARL. He had a thing.

MILES. Veruca?

CARL. A prior engagement.

MILES. You're worried we'd frighten him off?

CARL. I think he'd've been bored.

MILES. What does he do again, Carl?

JOHNNY. Miles, pack it in.

The women arrive, and kiss CARL.

MILES. I'm interested! Did you have to pretend you were drowning to get his attention? I mean, did he come down off his ladder and give you mouth to mouth?

CARL. We didn't meet at the pool.

MILES. In the locker room, then.

CARL. Yes.

MILES. God, it's so brilliantly predictable.

KITTY. As are you.

MILES. So, what, he just said – 'How about it'?

MILES *pours* CARL *a drink, refills his own glass.*

CARL. No. He said . . .

CARL *hesitates, self-conscious for a moment.*

(*Recalling, shyly moved.*) He said: 'Don't laugh, I think you're beautiful.'

The loveliness of it lands. The women 'ah . . . '

JOHNNY. Oh, I think that's rather good . . .

BEA. It's amazing.

MILES. Were you in your goggles?

BEA. Miles . . .

MILES. Look, I just think it's kind of fantastic. The way these guys get together on the basis of pure physical attraction and then spend the rest of the relationship wondering why they've got nothing in common and the thing never really works out.

JOHNNY. Cos straight people never do that.

CARL. We have stuff in common.

KITTY. You have loads in common.

MILES. Oh come on – you're a forty-something senior partner in a law firm, he's a twenty-something pool attendant!

CARL. But you know what I see when I look in his eyes?

MILES. The back of his head.

BEA. Miles!

CARL. Kindness, Miles.

JOHNNY. Kindness, Miles.

MILES. Fact remains, you've got a boyfriend whose neurone count doubles when he swallows a fly.

JOHNNY. Right – kitchen.

MILES *pulls a face.*

MILES. Blimey, here we go . . .

JOHNNY *spirits* MILES *away. We see them isolated for a moment.* MILES *pours himself another drink.*

So how come you're doing all the cooking? Kitty on strike?

JOHNNY. No, she cooked it, we're just carting it through.

MILES. Oh – I thought maybe . . .

JOHNNY. What?

MILES. You know, you earn a whack less than her now . . .

JOHNNY. It's not that much less actually. Teaching's better paid than people think.

MILES. Still, up against when you were still at the firm . . .

JOHNNY. Do you know what? It's just made no difference. Funny, that was the bit I was worried about but . . . we don't miss the money at all.

MILES. Hm.

MILES lifts a lid.

Peasant food.

JOHNNY. Moroccan.

MILES. I love how rich white people enjoy nothing better than a night indulging in foreign peasant food.

JOHNNY. We're not rich.

MILES. You aren't peasants.

JOHNNY. Don't eat it.

MILES. I'm starving. Besides, it smells great. What is that smell?

JOHNNY. Ras-al-Hanout.

MILES. Gesundheit.

JOHNNY (*needled, slightly holy tone*). It's a special blend, fifty-seven different spices.

MILES takes the hint.

MILES (*sincerely*). Wow.

But then:

I'll give you a tenner if you can name me two of them . . . ?

JOHNNY *turns, looking cross, but he's rumbled . . . starts to laugh. They return to the scene with the others, carrying appetizers.*

JOHNNY. I'm sorry, I'm bringing him back.

CARL. I don't care. He's just jealous.

KITTY. We're all jealous.

MILES. It's doomed is all I'm saying.

BEA. That's so negative . . .

MILES. Yes, but a relationship where you've no intellectual overlap is . . .

CARL. 'Intellectual overlap'?

MILES. Yes.

CARL. Miles, you're a prick.

MILES *smiles, pours another drink*. CARL *shakes his head*.

Okay. Tell me about your weekend so far then, you people with intellectual overlap.

KITTY. Oh – brace yourself, it's a whorl of sensation.

CARL. What were you doing last night, Bea?

BEA. Last night? Oh . . . Friday, so . . . Well, I got the kids to bed, and then watched a rerun of *Will and Grace* . . .

KITTY. Me too!

CARL. Okay – so you two have overlap but it's not that intellectual, and you're sadly not a couple. Next . . .

MILES. I hate *Will and Grace* . . .

JOHNNY. I hate it more. I hate it like poison.

CARL. Okay, see above. And so where are the men at this point on Friday . . . ?

MILES. I'm on the way home from a quick drink at the end of my arduous working week.

BEA. You can imagine how quick a drink that was. I see now how much Johnny kept Miles in check . . .

JOHNNY *hesitates*.

JOHNNY. And I'm watching *Will and Grace*.

The others laugh.

MILES. You fucking wuss, John.

JOHNNY. I'm tired and I'm doing some marking at the same time.

CARL. Right, so . . . ?

CARL cues BEA.

BEA. I go up to bed . . . well I'm whacked and I'm reading this book Kitty told me about . . .

KITTY. Oh . . . ?

CARL. Sure . . .

BEA. The French one.

CARL cues MILES.

MILES. And I get a takeaway.

KITTY. Have a bath.

BEA. I'd made dinner.

MILES. You don't *make* salad. It grows.

BEA. There was salad . . .

JOHNNY. I fall asleep over the marking, wake up on the sofa about two.

KITTY. I don't remember you coming up.

JOHNNY. Nor do I.

BEA. Saturday, I take Hettie to ballet.

KITTY. Cora to ballet.

MILES. Tommy to football.

JOHNNY. Tim to ju-jitsu.

BEA. Then I give the kids lunch . . . hand over to Miles . . .

KITTY (*'fessing up*). Pizza Express. Bad mother, bad mother.

JOHNNY. I successfully hook up the new WiFi system. Still have time left to play squash.

MILES. The Science Museum. Again.

KITTY. Then Johnny comes back.

JOHNNY. Via video shop. Some Pixar thing.

KITTY. I go to Waitrose.

BEA. To Tesco.

MILES. Bea can't park in the spaces at Waitrose.

BEA. I could park the Peugeot, the new one's too big . . .

JOHNNY. I give the kids tea so Kitty can pull in some time at her desk . . .

    KITTY *blows him a kiss, only semi-ironic.*

MILES. Your boss not coming back, Kit?

KITTY. Depends how it goes with the chemo.

BEA. What a shock . . . it began with a sore throat . . . ?

KITTY. Yeah . . .

BEA. God, frightening . . .

CARL *(censors, corrals)*. Bea – sorry – later . . . So . . . ?

BEA. Oh – oh, they get back, I give the kids tea, Miles goes to the offie. Though we've plenty of wine in.

MILES. Have a fag – sorry – smoke on the way – really living!

BEA. Kids to bed.

MILES. Sitter turns up.

BEA. Late.

MILES. And sulky, even though she's getting three times the national average to sit on our sofa watching pay-per-view movies on the plasma all night.

KITTY. Kids to bed. *Sleeping Beauty*. Start cooking.

JOHNNY. Start drinking.

Finally:

MILES. Finally – dinner with friends.

A mood of gloom settles. KITTY *grimaces.*

KITTY. Shit.

CARL. I want you to know that's much worse than I expected.

KITTY. It's awful.

JOHNNY. Okay, you've made your point, Carl. What were *you* up to?

CARL. Me . . . ?

MILES. Come on, Carlo, don't be a tease.

BEA. Make it dull so we can all feel better about ourselves . . .

CARL. Well Friday, we got invited to a thing at the zoo.

MILES. You went to the zoo?

MILES *pours more drinks, including for himself.*

JOHNNY. Sh.

CARL. It was a work dinner. We weren't going to go, cos it seemed so – well corporate, but I haven't been to the zoo in years and Antoniou's never been *here* so . . . I couldn't resist. And . . .

He's transported at the memory.

And it was amazing. Stunning . . .

(*He starts to draw them in.*) To be there at night, after lights out. All the animal smells and the strange squawks and howls, and the hot hungry little eyes glinting in the darkness . . .

BEA. Oh – I've got gooseflesh.

MILES. Bea, that's just the other lawyers.

But CARL *stares him down.*

CARL. No, Miles, it was incredible. And yes, of course there were all these buffoons in tuxes. But actually, that only made it more . . . surreal.

There was a full moon last night – none of you mentioned that . . . this blazing full moon . . . and they'd hired this string quartet . . . They were playing Elgar's 'Salut d'Amour' – do you know it? – it's very light, romantic . . . And I'd honestly assumed that the zoo would be sort of roped-off, I didn't think you'd be able to just wander around in the night . . . But we did . . .

He laughs at the recollection . . .

We could see ourselves there in the glass of the gorilla house . . . made long shadows across the penguin pond. It sounds silly . . .

BEA. No . . .

CARL. But it was magical. There were all these amazing things . . . coming alive. The nocturnal things you wait for and never see when the zoo's really open. Putting on a show just for us. I've got to tell you. It was quite extraordinary.

He sits back. The others absorb what he's described.

MILES. And then you went home and fucked like jack rabbits.

CARL *smiles*.

CARL. We went home. We made love. Went to bed.

KITTY. See, I like that: made love, went to bed. In that order.

JOHNNY. Yes – d'you have to be quite so sexually superior?

BEA. So what about today, Carl . . . ? What did you do today . . . ?

MILES. Bea, stop perving on Carl's life.

KITTY. It's okay, I do it all the time.

JOHNNY. No, Christ, come on. Let him finish what he's started.

CARL. Oh, well Toni was working this morning, so I slept in till nine or so . . .

KITTY (*to* BEA). 'Slept in' . . .

CARL. Then went down to meet him, had a swim and a steam.

Then we did the farmer's market, came home and he gave me a really fabulous massage . . .

MILES. *Then* you fucked like jack rabbits.

CARL. No . . .

BEA. Then they made love.

CARL. No.

KITTY and BEA are surprised.

KITTY. What then?

CARL. What 'what'?

The women are confused.

KITTY. Massage not followed by sex?

BEA shrugs, unable to comprehend.

CARL. So?

BEA gestures – surely it's clear.

MILES. Oh I see where this is going . . .

KITTY. Bea, when was the last time you had a massage not followed by sex?

MILES. Don't answer that. When did *you*?

KITTY (*unfazed by* MILES). At a spa a couple of years ago, but I half expected the girl to flip me over at the end, I've got so used to it . . .

JOHNNY wings a cushion at her, but they laugh.

CARL. Oh, thank God I'm me.

MILES. You're a shit-stirrer.

He points at CARL. We're struck by the fact that MILES is getting drunk.

He's enjoying this . . .

CARL. No, after the massage, I stayed in bed . . .

(*Shrugs, matter-of-fact.*) Toni made a salad, put the hoover round and emptied the dishwasher.

The women gasp.

MILES. I don't believe it.

KITTY (*still steeped in envy*). *I* don't believe it!

CARL *starts to laugh.*

BEA. He made that up!

KITTY. You bloody made that up, you bastard.

CARL *laughs more.*

I can't believe you'd do that!

CARL. Only the bit about the dishwasher!

MILES. The cunt.

CARL *looks at* MILES, *smiles.*

BEA. Miles.

MILES. Got the girls going though. He had you two right where he wanted you, though, the cunt . . .

JOHNNY. Miles, kitchen.

JOHNNY *stands, collects plates.*

MILES. Can't I just put some money in the swearbox?

JOHNNY. Up.

JOHNNY *hands* MILES *the plates, they head out together.*

KITTY (*calling after them*). Missing you already.

KITTY, CARL *and* BEA *laugh. We follow* MILES *and* JOHNNY *for a moment.*

MILES. That was pretty funny.

JOHNNY. Carl's on great form tonight.

MILES. I'm on to red.

> MILES *pours another glass of wine.*

> You?

JOHNNY. Why not.

> MILES *pours for* JOHNNY *too. Laughter breaks through for a second from the other room.*

> (*A tentative enquiry.*) You okay, Miles?

MILES. Sure . . . why . . . ?

JOHNNY. No. No reason.

MILES. Cheers.

> JOHNNY *nods.*

> Been a long week at work.

JOHNNY. Really?

MILES. I won't bore you with office politics. You've made your great escape.

JOHNNY. I wouldn't mind.

MILES. You're too nice, Johnny.

JOHNNY. No I'm not.

> MILES *laughs.*

MILES. Course you're not. Not underneath.

> *He starts to laugh again, entertaining himself.*

> Hey – Johnny – you know what Carl does to make Antoniou's eyes light up?

> JOHNNY *braces himself for the inevitable.*

JOHNNY. No.

MILES. Shines a torch in his ear . . . !

JOHNNY *laughs because he can't help it. We move back to* CARL *and the women.*

BEA. Poor Kitty. It must have been a shock.

KITTY. Yeah, more than you'd think. I mean, you reach an age where everyone's parents are getting ill and you ought to expect it . . .

CARL. But when it actually happens . . .

KITTY. Exactly. (*To* BEA.) And Dad and I haven't always got on that brilliantly.

BEA. Oh – I know things were . . .

KITTY. We didn't speak at all for a long time – years.

CARL. With good reason.

BEA. I think it is harder, when they're ill and the relationship's not . . . you know . . .

KITTY. And what makes it worse is I'm staying with Mum while I'm up there to visit him in hospital. So that rakes it all up again with her.

MILES *and* JOHNNY *return with red wine.*

MILES. What's getting raked up?

BEA. Kitty's dad.

MILES. What's happened to your dad?

JOHNNY. I told you.

MILES. Christ, yes – the leg off!

KITTY. It was only his foot, and they didn't amputate in the end, they managed to do this op and increase the blood supply . . .

MILES. Fantastic.

CARL. It's a weirdly violent idea, amputation.

KITTY. It is odd, isn't it, someone losing a big body part like that? You start to wonder what they'll do with it.

MILES. Whether you could keep it, turn it into an ashtray . . .

JOHNNY. And then there's all the shit with June. I mean, Kitty's mother an absolute vampire – she drains you bloody dry. I don't know how Kitty stands it. In fact I don't know how she *survived* it . . . God – and the thing with the phone!

CARL. Oh, the phone!

KITTY. You feel such a maniac having to tell the hospital, you know: 'If anything happens, this is the number I'm staying at, but you have to let it ring three times, then hang up and call again . . . '

MILES. What?

BEA. Oh, Kitty . . . not still . . .

    KITTY *nods*.

CARL. It's so sad.

JOHNNY. It's fucking bonkers.

MILES. You've lost me . . . at your mother's, you're saying . . .

BEA. She won't answer the phone . . .

JOHNNY. Or let *you* answer the phone . . .

KITTY. Unless the caller's rung three times and hung up, then called back.

JOHNNY. I won't do it.

CARL. Good for you.

    MILES *is bewildered*.

KITTY. But it's in this bloody dip, so I can't get a signal on the mobile.

MILES. Sorry – why the thing with the phone . . . ?

    KITTY *gestures*.

CARL. In case it's Kitty's dad.

MILES. But . . . but why would he be calling her . . . ? I mean, they split up, what . . . ?

KITTY. Nearly twenty years ago.

MILES. So does he call often?

KITTY. He's never called.

JOHNNY. Not once. Seemed perfectly happy all their married life, then walked out the week after Kitty left for college.

MILES. Someone else?

JOHNNY. Not as far as we know.

KITTY. I mean, there've been people since, but . . .

MILES. Just – out the door, and never looked back?

CARL. But June doesn't believe that!

KITTY. She won't give him the opportunity to get back in touch, she says. Wouldn't have him back if he got down on his knees and begged.

MILES (*slightly stunned by the story*). God.

JOHNNY. She thinks that's what he wants and she's holding him off.

KITTY. I don't think it's that simple, but . . .

MILES. Christ. It's depressing.

JOHNNY. It's really hard.

MILES. Shit. That is very depressing.

> MILES *pours more wine, drinks it, apparently genuinely depressed.*

CARL. You should refuse to collude with it. Just call her normally, and if she doesn't pick up . . .

JOHNNY. *I* do that. I won't give in to it.

KITTY. Well I tried, but she just lets it ring! And then she phones back to say Dad's been calling. I mean, you explain it was *you* but she insists it was him, and you just get dragged back into the whole fucking saga. I've given up.

MILES (*serious now*). She *wants* it to be him?

KITTY. I don't even know if that's true any more.

MILES (*considers further*). God, it's really a downer . . . does your dad know?

KITTY. No!

MILES. You ought to tell him.

KITTY. What for?

MILES (*sincere now*). You ought to tell him, Kitty.

The others are struck by his tone.

KITTY. Miles, I really don't have that kind of conversation with him, and I can't see what good it would . . .

MILES (*cuts her off, urgent*). You ought to tell him so he can ring three times, hang up, and ring back and say . . .

KITTY. Say what?

MILES *looks at* BEA.

MILES (*with terrible straightforward clarity*). Please let's stop this nonsense: I don't love you any more.

The table freezes. KITTY*'s voice comes up.*

KITTY'S VOICE. Long, long ago in a far away place . . . Long, long ago in a far away place . . . Long, long ago in a far away place . . . Long, long ago in a far away place . . .

During which, they peel off, one by one: first KITTY, *then* JOHNNY, CARL, BEA *and finally* MILES.

A telephone begins to ring.

Scene Four

The sound of a phone ringing. On an old-fashioned table, a lamp comes on beside a seventies' handset as it rings and rings.

KITTY*'s mother,* JUNE, *comes in, a neat, portly woman in late middle age.*

KITTY *stumbles in, wearing her dressing gown. She approaches the phone. Stands over it, worried. She is dreaming.*

JUNE. Let it go. I've learned to.

KITTY. I thought it might be the hospital.

JUNE. They'll ring back if it's anything important. You explained to them about . . . ?

She indicates the phone.

KITTY. Yes I explained. I explained.

JUNE. Well then.

A beat.

KITTY. You know that couldn't have been him – he's not well enough to make a phone call.

JUNE. Never underestimate your father, Kitty.

KITTY. Honestly. I saw him.

JUNE. He slept all through your visit, you said. He's probably feeling rested.

KITTY. He was still full of anaesthetic from the exploratory thing . . .

JUNE. I don't know. It's a shame. You came all this way. And he didn't even wake up. Typical.

KITTY. It's not that far.

JUNE. That's not what you usually say.

KITTY (*fortifies her defences*). This is different. This is serious.

JUNE. It's not what you said when I had that gastric scare.

KITTY. He's in hospital!

JUNE. The doctor said I should've been. She couldn't believe I'd got through it on my own. I told her – what choice do I have?

KITTY. They're going to amputate his foot.

JUNE *sighs*.

JUNE. Is my cough bothering you?

KITTY. I haven't heard you cough.

JUNE. I thought it might be keeping you awake.

KITTY. I haven't heard it.

JUNE. I've had it for months. Can't seem to shake it off. It's very worrying.

KITTY. Besides, I'm *working* upstairs, I told you.

JUNE. Busy busy.

KITTY. It's a busy time. With Stephanie off, I'm running the whole show. It's a lot of extra stuff.

JUNE. Mm. Turned out well for you, hasn't it?

KITTY *looks up in disbelief*.

KITTY. What?

JUNE. Well, you always said that should've been your job. She only beat you to it when you took the time off to have Cora.

KITTY. You understand Stephanie's *very* ill?

JUNE *frowns*.

JUNE. Quite odd, though, isn't it? Working for a cancer charity and then *getting* cancer.

KITTY *looks at her mother for a moment*.

KITTY. I think it's a coincidence.

JUNE. Still. At least she's got a diagnosis. They still can't say what's wrong with me.

She coughs, not that convincingly, for effect. KITTY *fights down a matricidal urge.*

KITTY. I'm . . .

She points back upstairs, starts away.

JUNE. Well don't worry about your father any more. He'll be alright.

KITTY (*controlled, corrective*). We don't know that.

JUNE. He won't have his foot off.

KITTY *can't help rising to the occasion.*

KITTY. Well he might, you know. He is in there on a ward with a bunch of other blokes who've already had theirs off.

JUNE *smirks.*

JUNE. I've known your father a very long time. I'd know if they were going to chop his foot off.

KITTY. You haven't seen him in so long . . . he's old, Mum.

JUNE. Makes no difference, believe you me. No, don't worry about him. He wouldn't worry about *you.*

KITTY. Don't say that. That's just a nasty thing to say . . .

JUNE. Look, I know this illness's brought you together.

KITTY. It's not 'brought us together'.

JUNE. I know he's phoned up and you think that . . . well . . . *means* something. But it doesn't.

KITTY. I don't think anything.

JUNE. That's good. Then you can't be disappointed. Because foot or no foot, your father won't change his ways . . .

KITTY. You need to stop doing that, just while he's ill . . .

JUNE. I've accepted it. It's time you did. That's why I couldn't ever have him back. I know that's what you wanted . . .

KITTY. No I didn't . . .

JUNE. I can tell sometimes you're angry with me because I wouldn't take him back.

KITTY. I promise you that's not true . . .

JUNE. But he'd only've done the same again. It's in his nature . . .

KITTY. Stop this. Please.

JUNE (*completely ignores* KITTY *again*). No question. You know what I always say: why did your father cross the road . . . ?

She sighs, gestures despair, begins to move offstage. KITTY *comes up with the answer just as her mother is disappearing.*

KITTY *and* JUNE. Because he thought the chicken was a slut.

The phone begins to ring again . . . KITTY *looks at it.* JUNE *looks round.* KITTY *hesitates – torn between her mother and the phone. Finally, she turns and walks away leaving it ringing.* JUNE *absorbs her daughter's decision, reassured. Goes off. A* GIRL'S VOICE *comes up, singing a playground song . . .*

GIRL'S VOICE.
    My boyfriend gave me an apple
    My boyfriend gave me a pear . . .

Scene Five

KITTY*'s kitchen. The song continues, indistinct in the background, as* JOHNNY *rushes in, coat on, carrying his briefcase.*

JOHNNY (*shouting – loudly*). Now, Tim! We are very very very late.

    KITTY *rushes in, still wearing her dressing gown. She carries two kids' lunchboxes and a bag of satsumas.*

KITTY. Shit shit shit.

JOHNNY. Your gym just called. They say it's three months since you joined and you haven't been in yet.

KITTY. Bastards. God, I wish Cora would –

(Shrieking offstage.) – stop singing that song!

She pushes a satsuma into each lunchbox.

JOHNNY *(with a hostile agenda)*. Are you alright?

KITTY. No. I had a terrible night. I was dreaming and I can't remember what about. So now I'm in a bad mood and I can't remember why.

JOHNNY. Great.

She closes the lunchboxes, gives them to JOHNNY.

KITTY. Then the loaf had gone mouldy for the kids' lunchboxes and I had to put ricecakes in, so Cora's had a hissy fit and Tim's in a sulk. I couldn't find the satsumas I bought and remembered they were still in the car, so I went out to get the damn things and I've stepped in this pile of dogshit in my flipflops.

JOHNNY *(squaring up)*. Okay – Cora says you called her a 'bloody brat'.

KITTY *gasps at the betrayal.*

KITTY. God, the little snitch!

JOHNNY. Well do you think it's appropriate?

KITTY. Of course I don't!

JOHNNY. You shouldn't swear at her, Kitty.

KITTY. Did she actually say 'bloody' to you . . . ? She did, didn't she? I'm going to . . .

JOHNNY. Hey – *you're* the one in the wrong here, not her.

(Screaming offstage.) Tim, get down here or we're going without you!

KITTY. What?!

JOHNNY. She's *five*.

KITTY. And she knows what words are banned! She said it to wind you up and get you to have a go at me and you've risen – if I may say so – rather brilliantly to the bait!

He gathers up the lunchboxes.

JOHNNY. I haven't got time now, we'll talk about it later.

KITTY. No we won't! I'm not a kid in your class, John. I'm her mother.

JOHNNY. That doesn't mean it's okay for you to swear at her!

KITTY. No, but it makes it a fat sight more fucking likely that I'll want to! And could you maybe get off my back? I'm punching well above my weight at this euthanasia seminar in a hour and a half on the other side of town and I can't pick up the notes that I emailed myself from work yesterday because the frigging WiFi's down. I also can't pick up the list of other participants, so in a nutshell I've got a morning where I have no idea what I'm talking about or to whom and there's dogshit between my toes. And the last thing I need is a lecture from you about swearing at Cora! And she *was* being a brat!

JOHNNY. God, I'm so sick of leaving for work in this desperate exhausted state every day!

KITTY. Are you competing with me on the tiredness thing?

JOHNNY. No . . .

KITTY. Good because I'm on my knees!

JOHNNY. I'm late back tonight.

KITTY. What . . . ?

JOHNNY. PSA liaison – I told you.

(*Bellows offstage before she can respond.*) Tim, for crying out loud!

Goes off. KITTY*'s alone. Breathes a second . . .*

KITTY. Oh God, give me strength, give me strength, give me strength . . .

The GIRL'S VOICE *comes up clear, echoing in* KITTY*'s head . . .*

GIRL'S VOICE.

My boyfriend gave me an apple

My boyfriend gave me a pear . . .

My boyfriend gave me a kiss on the lips

So I threw him down the stairs . . .

KITTY *braces against the song, then she goes.*

KITTY (*shouting*). Tim, you're making Dad late again!!!

Scene Six

JOHNNY*'s school/seminar venue.* JOHNNY *rushes in, dumps his briefcase and begins squeaking up the words 'THE COMMA' on a white board.*

JOHNNY. Good morning, 4R.

He imitates the sing-song parodic response as he gets a sheaf of papers out his briefcase.

Good mor-ning, Mr Warr-ing-ton . . .

Okay – I've marked yesterday's homework on onomatopoeia – words that sound like the things they describe . . . and some of these responses are very good.

He looks through the papers . . .

'Rustle', 'splash' and 'crunch' – three excellent choices. What've we here . . . ? 'Bang', 'crash' and 'wallop' – not sure about 'wallop' but you possibly know better than I do. 'Squish', 'drip' and 'crack' – very good, very good. And the person who wrote 'department', 'cheese' and 'sceptical' needs to see me after class.

Okay – today we're talking about the uses and abuses of
the comma and why it is such an important element of
punctuation. So take out your literacy workbooks and we'll
get started.

JOHNNY *turns and writes on the board: 'Mr Warrington
says Mrs Ali is the best teacher in the school.'*

As JOHNNY*'s writing,* MICHAEL *strides on downstage and
waves out front. At the same time* KITTY *crosses upstage in
the opposite direction, sees* MICHAEL *– is horrified. He continues off, she hurries off in the opposite direction.*

(*Turning back.*) Right. Well words are shifty unreliable
toerags that don't mean the same thing from one moment to
the next, so we use different strategies for working out what
they mean at any given time. *Today* we're going to learn
about using *commas* to make sure we've got our words
under control.

Let's look now at the sentence on the board: 'Mr Warrington
says Mrs Ali is the best teacher in the school.' Ah, aren't I
nice? But wait . . . here come two commas . . .

JOHNNY *inserts the commas. The sentence now reads: 'Mr
Warrington, says Mrs Ali, is the best teacher in the school.'*

Yes – exactly. 'Mr Warrington, says Mrs Ali, is the best
teacher in the school.' Very different. Let's try some more . . .

*He starts to write: 'Kitty says Johnny is selfish.' 'Nietzsche
says God is dead.'*

KITTY *comes in, furtive, upset, on her phone . . .*

KITTY. Carl Potter, please . . .

Well is he really in a meeting or just . . .

With a client or a colleague . . . ?

It's just it's urgent . . .

Sure . . . can you tell him it's me. I'm on the mobile . . . and –
can you tell him it's an emergency . . . ?

She hangs up – sees MICHAEL *beginning to cross back over the space.*

Shit.

KITTY *hides behind the whiteboard.* MICHAEL *heads off.*

JOHNNY *finishes writing.*

JOHNNY. So copy them into your exercise books and see if you can turn the meaning around using just two commas . . . You've got two minutes, then I'll be coming around to check.

He pushes off the whiteboard, revealing KITTY. KITTY'*s phone rings.*

KITTY. Oh – Carl!

CARL *enters.*

CARL (*worried, on his phone*). Are you okay?

KITTY. Yes – I don't know – I don't think so . . .

CARL. What is it . . . ?

KITTY. He's here . . .

CARL. Who?

KITTY. The guy – creepy sadsack . . . He's here at this seminar.

CARL. That's your emergency?

KITTY. It's just I . . . I saw him, and panicked . . . Carl . . . I don't know what's wrong with me . . .

CARL. Kit, you just pulled me out of briefing a client for a tribunal at ten . . .

KITTY. Oh I'm sorry . . . I'm sorry, I just feel so . . . unsteady . . .

CARL. 'Unsteady'?

KITTY. I'm maybe just tired . . .

CARL. What's the guy got to do with it?

KITTY. He just . . . he unnerved me . . .

CARL. You're letting him mindfuck you.

KITTY. Am I? Is that it? He's very intense. He kind of locks on . . .

CARL. Well don't let him!

KITTY. I tell you, he'll do some big number. I mean, he's obsessive. It's like getting hypnotised by the snake in *The Jungle Book* with the whirly-whirly eyes . . .

CARL. Kitty, stop! For heaven's sake . . .

KITTY. I'm sorry. You're right. Look, I'll try and avoid him.

CARL. Don't avoid him, just deal with him! Do your job.

KITTY. Well of course, it's not really my job . . .

CARL. And it never will be if you don't get a grip.

KITTY. Don't say that . . . Stephanie might get well, she might come back.

She looks off to where she last saw MICHAEL.

Oh shit . . . he's a beast, Carl, I'm telling you . . .

CARL. Look, I've got to get back in this meeting. But just be clear with the guy, you know. Warn him off: you're meeting him here in a professional context and you expect him to behave in a professional way. Now, I'll call you later.

He starts walking offstage.

KITTY. Okay, you're right . . . sorry, Carl . . . I'm so sorry, I'll let you . . .

But now MICHAEL*'s back and heading straight towards her.* KITTY*'s transfixed.*

. . . get back.

CARL*'s gone now. And* MICHAEL *just keeps coming.*

(*To herself.*) Shit. Right . . .

KITTY *hangs up the phone, steels herself as* MICHAEL*'s approaching, opts to take the initiative, her attitude heavily defended.*

Well . . . How are *you*?

MICHAEL *smiles, shakes her hand warmly, hardly inter-
rupting his walk.*

MICHAEL. Hey – Michael Manson, Age Awareness . . .

KITTY. I remember . . .

MICHAEL. – nice to see you . . .

*He touches her arm very briefly, a politician's glancing grace,
as he breaks away and heads straight off.*

KITTY *is left alone. She looks after where he's gone, struggling to absorb what just passed between them.*

The hospital monitor comes up – beep, beep, beep, beep . . .

KITTY *remains where she is but gradually finds herself –
somewhat disoriented – in:*

Scene Seven

BEA *and* MILES' *kitchen. Tester-pot patches, barely distin-
guishable from one another, all over the back wall. A large polythene sheet hanging across the room.*

MILES. Welcome – this is Bea's tester-pot painting. 'A life lived
in neutral . . . ', I call it. I'm thinking of offering it to Tate
Modern. What d'you reckon?

JOHNNY. You could have come to us.

BEA. We *owed* you.

MILES. And we need you to come and be interesting. Bring a bit
of the world in.

BEA. Give me your coats . . .

She waits a beat, before:

Kitty?

KITTY (*coming to*). Sorry . . . miles away . . .

> KITTY *hands* BEA *her coat.* BEA *goes out with them.*
> MILES *pours drinks from a jug – mojitos.*

JOHNNY. God, you look so well, Miles . . .

MILES. Mm?

JOHNNY. It's just annoying you live this life of almost complete dissipation and you look like you've just stepped off a yacht.

MILES. In the garden a bit last weekend. P'raps that's it.

> BEA *comes back.*

KITTY. It's nice of you to ask *Carl*.

BEA. Oh – are you sure?

KITTY. Yes, of course!

BEA. I mean, I know he's *your* friend.

KITTY. It's great.

MILES. Bea thought it'd give you someone to talk to. Toni's at some club. Don't know if it's a 'club' club or a *club* club.

KITTY. No . . .

MILES. I'll get the kids settled in.

JOHNNY. I'll give you a hand. Cora's already in her pyjamas.

KITTY. Or I can . . . I don't mind?

> *But they're already on the way out.*

MILES. No – stay with Bea. Help her with her great dilemma.

> *The men go.*

KITTY. What dilemma?

BEA. It's nothing. He means the paint colours.

> *The doorbell rings.*

> Oh . . .

KITTY nods as BEA excuses herself. Alone, KITTY considers the wall. CARL enters bearing wine and flowers.

Oh, Carl, you're all wet.

CARL. I know.

BEA. The others didn't get wet.

CARL. No.

BEA. They just arrived a minute ago and they didn't get wet.

CARL. What can I say?

BEA. What lovely flowers.

CARL. You're very welcome.

BEA. Let's take this jacket . . . I hope it's not spoiled . . .

CARL. Me too . . .

BEA. They are beautiful. You have such good taste.

KITTY. You should get Carl to help with your pressing dilemma.

BEA. That's a great idea . . .

She heads out with his coat. CARL smiles winningly after her.

CARL. What dilemma?

KITTY. Pick a shade of pale. Look, we've got linen, stone, beige, bone, blossom, dove, vanilla, biscuit . . .

He cringes at the patchy wall.

CARL. Dear God – that's a cry for help . . . Why have you brought me here . . . ?

KITTY. We'll have a nice time.

CARL. Right.

KITTY. They're happier than you think they are.

CARL. There are lobsters in restaurant tanks happier than I think they are. Can they cook at least?

KITTY. We're getting takeaway.

CARL. You're joking . . .

KITTY. The builders disconnected the cooker or something, so they've ordered from the Thai place round the corner. It's fabulous actually.

CARL. And how are you?

KITTY. Oh – fine!

CARL. Yeah . . . ? Feeling steady?

KITTY. As a rock. I'm so sorry about . . .

CARL. No, no – just bad timing. I called you back all afternoon but you never picked up.

KITTY. You know what? – my phone was flat.

CARL. I started to get worried. In case he'd white-slaved you.

KITTY. Nothing like that.

CARL. So it went okay – you saw him off?

KITTY. It went great, I did fine.

CARL. Attagirl.

BEA *returns*.

KITTY. I was just telling Carl how great this Thai place is.

BEA. Well I would've cooked . . . we've got this two-ring hob thing I get by on, but . . .

MILES *enters with* JOHNNY.

MILES. But Miles said no, let's get some takeaway.

BEA. We've over-ordered – we always do – but it's better to have too much, don't you think . . .

MILES. Too much is not enough. I've stocked up on this lovely Alsacian white to go with. Carlo – mojito?

CARL. *Porque non?*

MILES *pours a drink for* CARL.

BEA. He drank most of the wine before you got here.

JOHNNY. Always the selfless host.

MILES. You know I actually used to worry about drinking to excess. I didn't understand why I did it, and that bothered me.

JOHNNY. But now you do?

MILES. The simplest thing, John – it makes me feel alive.

BEA. I imagine people are thinking it's a shame you can't find anything else to make you feel alive, Miles.

MILES. Well, I can, of course.

KITTY. Like what?

MILES. Oh, I swear by the same three things that keep most people going: drinking, fucking and telling lies. It's almost evidence of a beneficent universe that they combine to such fantastic effect.

KITTY. Telling lies?

MILES. Oh yes, Kitty: the moment you tell a lie, you begin a story – it's a whole new set of possibilities. I've only to indulge in the palest of porkies to feel I've been given a last-minute pardon, flooded with a hot surge of bright potential. You ought to try it sometime.

He looks at BEA.

Oh – look at Bea's face. Bea, you look like you're trying to poo out a pine cone. Backwards. Grab another bottle out of the fridge, John, and I'll dust off the glasses . . .

BEA. I dusted them . . .

(*To* KITTY.) It gets everywhere.

KITTY. I'm sure. You're very brave.

BEA. It'll be worth it when it's finished.

BEA *spots* JOHNNY *looking confused.*

Oh Johnny, it's behind the sheet thing . . .

JOHNNY. Got it.

JOHNNY *battles through the polythene sheet to get at the fridge.*

MILES. If it's ever finished.

BEA. It's actually right on schedule. Within the bounds of the contingency. When I drew up the contract I put in a series of penalty clauses.

CARL. Good for you, Bea.

BEA. You've got to or they ride roughshod. Miles doesn't know these things. It's my project.

CARL. Bea's very sensible to draw up a proper contract.

MILES. If you say so, Carl.

BEA (*squaring up*). He does say so, he just did. He's a lawyer.

CARL *and* KITTY *try to smile.* JOHNNY*'s back from behind the polythene sheet. He has a sheet of paper in his hand. He's not happy.*

JOHNNY. Miles . . . ?

MILES. What . . . ?

JOHNNY. This, stuck on the fridge . . .

BEA (*seeing*). Oh . . .

MILES. Shit . . .

MILES *sighs.*

KITTY. What is it?

JOHNNY. It's term dates for St Margaret's. With Hettie's name at the top.

KITTY*'s surprised . . . a sudden chill runs through the room.*

KITTY. You're not thinking of moving Hettie . . . ?

JOHNNY. They're not thinking of moving her, they've term dates, it's a done deal, right?

JOHNNY*'s stunned, very upset.*

MILES. John, I was going to tell you . . . I feel bad about it – nothing personal . . .

JOHNNY. Nothing personal?

MILES. The thing is that Hettie is gifted.

BEA. *Officially* gifted. They tested her.

JOHNNY. Oh – did they?

MILES. Bea felt she needed stretching . . .

JOHNNY. And you think a *church* school's going to *stretch* her . . . ?

BEA. Their results are fantastic.

JOHNNY. Well of course they are, Bea! They select their fucking students!

KITTY. Johnny . . . it's nothing to do with us really –

JOHNNY. For Christ's sake! It's my school they're pulling her out of!

BEA. You've only just started there . . .

JOHNNY. And she's my goddaughter!

MILES. You don't believe in God!

JOHNNY. Nor do you.

CARL. Nor do I but it scares me when everyone says it out loud . . .

KITTY. Please – let's stop this . . .

JOHNNY (*inconsolable*). No! – I'm appalled! I'm . . . I'm amazed and appalled. I don't know what to say.

BEA. It was a very difficult decision . . .

JOHNNY. Well coming from someone who's been struggling to choose between beige and off-white for six months, that's not the *cri de cœur* you might imagine!

CARL. Hey Johnny, come on . . .

But JOHNNY*'s anger is building not subsiding.*

JOHNNY. Christ, look at the world we live in! And our friends're taking their daughter out of a school where she sits side by side with her neighbourhood peers of various abilities and ethnic origins and spiritual persuasions, to have her dripfed mindless superstition and prejudice in a sectarian crammer! What fucking hope is there for any of us?

BEA. They sing 'All Things Bright and Beautiful' once a week, it's hardly . . .

KITTY. Please, John . . .

BEA. You're overreacting.

JOHNNY. Am I? You know St Margaret's head of science is Pentecostal? I mean, they do creationism alongside the flash in the pan that is Darwin.

BEA. Het's a bright girl, she'll see through all that.

JOHNNY. And what will you tell her when she asks you why you've got a pervert like Carl round to dinner?

KITTY. Enough now!

JOHNNY. No . . .

CARL. It's fine.

JOHNNY. . . . . I mean, that's the Pentecostal party line, right? Pervert and abomination.

CARL. Last time I checked.

MILES. We'll say we're unbelievably charitable and hoping to cure him.

CARL. By example, I'm guessing.

MILES. Exactly: present him with a vision of heterosexual contentment so fucking complete he won't be tempted to fall back on his felching ways.

JOHNNY. What about the kids like Carl in that school . . .

KITTY. John . . .

JOHNNY. When Carl told his dad he was gay, his dad was sick on him. *On* him!

BEA. That's enough . . .

JOHNNY. No . . .

KITTY (*to* CARL). I'm sorry.

JOHNNY. You know what Voltaire said?

MILES. It's on the tip of my tongue.

JOHNNY. He said, 'As long as men believe absurdities they are condemned to commit atrocities.' You're sending her to a school where the teaching of absurdities is the highest priority! Miles, how could you?

MILES. It's Bea's bloody idea.

BEA. You're giving everybody a false impression . . .

MILES. I'm not pushy at all. I'd be delighted if both kids turned out to be dimmer than me. Who wants to be outshone by their offspring?

BEA. Well you heard him . . . ! That's what I'm up against! The kids need some kind of stability. They need *some* moral frame of reference.

JOHNNY. Couldn't they maybe get that from you, Bea? I mean, I'm not sure you're meant to contract out that part of the relationship.

MILES. Bloody good point.

BEA (*standing firm*). It's been decided. They'll teach her a way of seeing things, of how to understand things.

JOHNNY. So would I.

BEA. Based on what?

JOHNNY (*snaps*). Well I could say, based on the great fruits of the Enlightenment, Bea – y'know, common sense, decency, reason, compassion, but since we've been friends for the last twenty years, I'm not sure I should dignify that with a response!

KITTY. John, calm down . . .

JOHNNY. No – what am I? – nothing?

BEA. This isn't about you.

JOHNNY. Really . . . ?

MILES. Johnny, don't . . .

JOHNNY. Is this not about me, Miles . . . ? Miles . . . ?

MILES *doesn't answer. He looks away. A yawning stand-off between the men now.*

KITTY. Look . . .

JOHNNY. Get the coats and the kids, yeah?

KITTY. Johnny . . .

JOHNNY. Can you just . . . ?

KITTY *yields.*

MILES. Kitty – no . . .

But CARL *and* KITTY *are on the way out.*

JOHNNY. Okay – I'm going to say it.

MILES. Don't. Whatever it is.

JOHNNY. I'm going to say it because I have to say one true incontrovertible thing before I leave.

BEA. Just go, Johnny.

JOHNNY. Your daughter's not gifted.

BEA. Just get out.

JOHNNY. I love Hettie, I do . . . she's a wonderful wonderful
girl, and it's been my privilege to know her and watch her
grow up, but trust me, she's not fucking gifted!

BEA *looks homicidal.*

MILES. Shit. You probably do have to get out now.

KITTY *enters.*

KITTY. John?

JOHNNY *shakes his head, exhausted.* KITTY *puts her arm
round him, leads him to the door. She looks back for a
second, then they're gone.*

BEA *and* MILES *in horrible silence.*

KITTY *appears, in a separate space, takes off her coat.*
JOHNNY *enters behind her –*

I'll make some pasta.

JOHNNY *nods.*

You look shakey.

JOHNNY. I'm fine.

He looks at her.

KITTY. I don't know what to say, John.

JOHNNY. He's still pissed off because I left. He's jealous I got
out. This is just to punish me. People don't like it when you
make a change. They find it very challenging.

KITTY *shrugs. Maybe.*

I'll give Carl a hand with the kids, yeah?

KITTY *nods. He goes.* KITTY *looks at her surroundings.*
CARL's *voice comes up* . . .

CARL'S VOICE. Long, long ago in a far away place lived a
kind king and queen who had everything they wished for
except for the thing they wanted the most . . . a fifty-inch
Bang & Olufsen wrap-around sound, HD-ready flatscreen TV.

KITTY *sits, braced for trouble . . .*

After a few seconds, MILES *and* BEA's *doorbell.*

BEA. Don't get it.

MILES *stands up.*

Don't get it! I don't want them back in here.

MILES *ignores her, goes out. Returns with two carrier bags full of takeaway food. Plonks them on the table.*

MILES. Well you really are the hostess with the mostest tonight, Bea.

MILES *sits with his drink again, stares into the middle distance.* BEA *watches a moment, then dumps the dinner in the bin.* MILES *is unmoved. After a while:*

BEA. Can you see me, Miles? I mean, can you even see me any more?

MILES *looks at her, considers, shrugs.*

MILES. No.

He takes a drink.

Yet, oddly, it doesn't feel like such a loss. I mean, I'm not down at the quack's begging for laser surgery, am I? Or a puff of marijuana to turn back time.

BEA *shakes her head . . . a new resolve forming . . .*

BEA. Miles, I know you're drunk . . . and I know that in the morning you won't remember this. And I know that if you could remember it, you'd be sorry for the sheer . . . sheer nastiness of it . . . but . . . I'm warning you – if you say one more stupidly pointlessly viciously unkind thing to me tonight, that will be it.

He looks at her.

You'll have to go and not come back . . . Do you understand, Miles? One more pathetic snipe and that's it.

MILES *considers a moment, calculates.*

MILES (*slowly, deliberately*). Do you know, Bea . . . I think . . .
if women were dominoes . . . you'd be the double bloody
blank.

*The hospital monitor beeps once more, then flatlines, all
alarms squealing.* KITTY *closes her eyes.*

Blackout.

End of Act One.

ACT TWO

Scene Eight

MILES – *more or less as before, except now he's standing in* JOHNNY *and* KITTY*'s kitchen.* KITTY *as before, but with a suitcase beside her, her jacket over it. She's just got home.* JOHNNY *looks on.*

MILES. You won't know you've got me. Truly, Kitty. Truly.

KITTY. Okay, Miles.

He kisses both her hands, penitential.

MILES. I don't know what I've done to deserve you. Something I can't remember.

KITTY. Something I can't remember either.

He laughs.

MILES. One in a million.

He embraces her.

Right – I'll leave you to it. You won't know I'm here.

MILES *goes out. A couple of moments pass before* KITTY *explodes at* JOHNNY *as quietly as she can.*

KITTY. How did this happen? I mean, how is it possible that this happened? That I went away and had this just *awful* time and then came back to Miles moved in?

JOHNNY. The timing's not ideal, I know.

KITTY. Ideal!

JOHNNY. I *know*, Kit.

KITTY. And you didn't think to call me? To warn me?

JOHNNY. I did call but – oh, guess what? – no one picked up . . .

KITTY. Oh, for fuck's sake . . .

JOHNNY. Look – it only happened yesterday. Someone from the firm rang and told me Miles was sleeping in the office, I had no choice.

KITTY *shakes her head, struggles to take in the information.*

KITTY. So where's he sleeping now?

JOHNNY. In the spare room.

KITTY. We haven't got a spare room.

JOHNNY. In the study.

KITTY. Shit and piss, John! Shit and piss. You *know* how much work I'm doing at home these days . . . ! *And* you!

JOHNNY. Sh . . .

KITTY. Don't shush me!

JOHNNY. You'll wake the kids.

KITTY. That's not true. You just don't want Miles to hear. I cannot believe it – I went away for two days –

JOHNNY. It was a long two days.

KITTY. I think I know how long it's been, Johnny! My dad just had an aortal aneurysm! I mean, an aortal fucking aneurysm! Do you know what happens when your aorta *bursts*, do you? I mean, he actually died and they brought him back to life! They don't know how they did it. Do you have any idea what that's . . . what it's like . . . ? God!

JOHNNY. Don't wake the children! It took an hour to get them down tonight.

KITTY. It always does, it's just it's usually *my* hour.

JOHNNY. I'm trying to do the right thing here!

KITTY. So how long is he staying?

JOHNNY. I don't know . . . it's hard to tell what's . . .

KITTY *shakes her head.*

KITTY. Christ.

Do you have any idea what I've been through . . . ?

JOHNNY. Look, Kit, I'm sorry – but it's not like I really know your dad . . .

KITTY. Oh – well, that makes it okay then. In fact, it actually gives us something in common. And yes – he's stable. Thanks for asking. Even Miles asked, John.

JOHNNY. I said I was sorry.

KITTY *breathes, struggles to come to terms.*

KITTY. I can't believe this . . . I mean, I told you I've been feeling unsteady . . .

JOHNNY. No you didn't.

KITTY. Yes I did!

JOHNNY. When?

KITTY (*remembering*). No, I didn't . . . I told Carl.

JOHNNY. Oh – great!

KITTY. Yeah – he can actually find time to speak to me.

JOHNNY. Well what would you like me to do, Kitty, ask the class to read quietly for a minute while you and I have a heart to heart? I'm sorry but in the real world there just isn't time to all sit round discussing our emotions.

KITTY. Jesus! Why are you being like this?

JOHNNY. Because I'm stretched too bloody thin!

KITTY. And whose fault's that . . . ? The whole point of this great career change was to do something that didn't completely dominate your life. To give you more time for the family.

JOHNNY. Hey – it's a real job, Kit. I'm not some housewife with a hobby! And the point was to do something *useful*. Something where I actually – excuse me, but – made some tiny positive contribution to the world.

KITTY. Well thank God I'm only trying to find a cure for cancer!

KITTY *shakes her head, demoralised.*

JOHNNY. Look – I wish I could have come with you. I feel really bad about it, but . . .

KITTY. Sorry, Johnny, but in the real world there just isn't time to all sit round discussing our emotions.

I'm going to bed.

She starts towards the door.

JOHNNY. You should've said you felt unsteady. I need to know these things . . . I never know what you're thinking . . .

She's almost out the door, when she stops, looks back:

KITTY. Okay, I'm thinking: is this my life? My one and only life? This fucking chaos of miscommunication and petty resentment and kids I only half-recognise and mouldy bread and dogshit and cancer and burst aortas and the fitness police and your alcoholic development-arrested friends and my evil fucking mother? Is this *it*?

KITTY *shakes her head, then she's gone. A few moments, then* MILES *comes back in.*

MILES. Everything okay?

JOHNNY *struggles to recover.*

JOHNNY. Yeah – yeah, it's fine.

MILES. Kitty not humpy?

JOHNNY. Just tired from the drive.

MILES. Good her old boy pulled through.

JOHNNY. Yeah.

MILES. D'you want me to sit the kids while the two of you go out?

JOHNNY. Oh – thanks, but I've got work to catch up on before morning. And Kit will have too.

MILES. Right.

JOHNNY's quiet.

She's a lovely person, Kit.

JOHNNY. Yeah.

MILES. I could have been kinder with someone like Kit. You can't be kind to Bea. She's just one of those people you want to be cruel to.

Beat.

Johnny, I was thinking – tomorrow, we could let Kitty watch *Will and Grace*. You know, as a gesture.

JOHNNY looks up at MILES' genuinely expectant face.

JOHNNY. Yeah.

MILES. She'd like that.

JOHNNY. Yeah.

MILES gives JOHNNY the thumbs-up. Great. The sound of a monitor beeping, a steady rhythm.

Scene Nine

JUNE's house – the lamp, the phone, the whole dreamscape. JUNE comes in.

JUNE. He's not going to die.

No response.

(*Calling off.*) I said: he's not going to die.

KITTY *comes in, exhausted, in her dressing gown. She carries two mugs of tea.*

KITTY. The consultant says the first six hours are crucial. We've still got two to go.

JUNE. Well you know what . . .

KITTY (*snaps*). Don't do it! Don't do the thing where you say: 'Your father won't die, he wouldn't give you the satisfaction' – just don't do it!

JUNE (*hurt*). I wasn't going to!

KITTY *breathes.*

KITTY. Good.

JUNE. I was going to say we'll sit them out together, the two hours.

KITTY. Oh . . .

JUNE. Two hours is a long time . . . when you're waiting . . . on your own.

I should know.

KITTY. How's your tea?

JUNE *looks at the cup, anxious.*

JUNE. Have you washed your hands since you got back? I don't want that hospital superbug.

KITTY *looks hostile.*

(*Defending herself.*) I have to look out for myself. You don't know what it's like.

KITTY *drinks her tea.* JUNE *follows suit. Winces as she sips.* KITTY *sees. After a while:*

KITTY. What?

JUNE. Nothing.

KITTY *watches, wary.* JUNE *sighs, regretful. Sips and winces again.*

KITTY. What?!

JUNE *shakes her head.*

JUNE (*with some sincerity*). Poor Kitty.

I mean, first of all your father's aorta bursts and then you've got me with this *awful* toothache.

KITTY. What toothache?

JUNE. It's most likely an abscess forming. You know they say there's no pain like toothache.

KITTY *tries to screen out her mother.*

(*Persisting.*) It's the kind of pain where you feel like your cheek should be puffed out to *here*. Then you look in the mirror and . . . nothing. You get no sympathy. Of course, that's the worst kind of abscess, where it doesn't puff out. That means the pain's trapped. The pressure building . . .

KITTY. You know they said it was a miracle Dad survived what happened. A miracle, they said.

JUNE (*shrugs*). Well, Barbara Kirby's sister's had what he's had and she's fit as a flea these days. Mind you, she takes care of herself.

KITTY. Who's Barbara Kirby?

JUNE. You know – Jamie Robertson's mother's sister.

KITTY. Who's Jamie Robertson?

JUNE. Jamie *Robertson*. They lived round the corner before we moved here. He had three nipples.

KITTY*'s bewildered.*

He was the year below you at school, you must remember . . . a chubby boy – well, his mother worked . . .

KITTY. What?

JUNE. She didn't cook properly – I don't blame her, she didn't have time.

KITTY *steels herself to let this go.*

His mother's sister – Barbara. She had what your father's got.
Now she sleeps with a little pyramid on her bedside table.
She pours a glass of water every night, sets it down under the
pyramid and in the morning, when she wakes up, the water's
full of bubbles.

KITTY*'s losing the will to live.*

KITTY. Okay.

JUNE. Fit as a flea – she's on the toy bus now for Belarus.

KITTY. The what?

JUNE. Belarus. In South America.

KITTY. Belarus isn't in South America.

JUNE. Central America, then.

KITTY. You mean Belize.

JUNE. Be-la-roose.

KITTY (*raising her voice, exasperated*). I know –

JUNE. Don't snap!

KITTY (*calming down*). I know you mean Belarus. Look –

(*Abandons the idea of further explanation.*) Never mind.
Whatever.

Beat.

JUNE (*looking at her watch*). Well that's two minutes gone.

KITTY (*getting up*). I'm going to try and do some work, distract
myself . . .

And Belarus is in Eastern Europe. Former Soviet bloc.

JUNE. If you say so.

KITTY. Not 'If I say so' – it's somewhere near the Ukraine –
they got all the spill from Chernobyl.

JUNE (*sighs*). Don't you get sick of being right all the time, Kitty?

KITTY *laughs*.

Must drive Johnny round the bend.

KITTY *stops laughing*.

KITTY. I can't say he's ever mentioned it.

JUNE. No, well, that's what he's like, isn't it?

KITTY. What?

JUNE. Still waters.

KITTY*'s wrongfooted for a moment* . . .

KITTY. What d'you mean by that?

JUNE. Nothing. No, no question, you've got a good one there.

Mind you, that's what I thought.

KITTY *shakes her head, about to walk away again, but then the phone begins to ring.* KITTY *looks at the phone. It continues, horribly insistent.* KITTY *and* JUNE *look at one another. The phone rings and rings and rings and rings . . . Eventually it stops.* KITTY *breathes. Tries to collect herself.*

KITTY. Right. Well I ought to . . .

JUNE. Wait, I've got something for you.

KITTY. I don't want it.

JUNE. It's *yours*. You loved it . . .

KITTY *glances back.* JUNE *holds out a skinny plastic doll.* JUNE *waggles it.*

KITTY. A Barbie?

JUNE. Sindy. Like Barbie but cheaper. I was looking out some things for Belarus and there she was . . .

JUNE *waves the doll.* KITTY *goes back, takes it, examines it.*

KITTY. I'm sorry, I don't remember her.

JUNE (*swallowing her disappointment*). Oh. Well . . . that's life, isn't it? All the happy times, all the love and attention and self-sacrifice for your children. And they don't remember any of it. Yours'll be the same – you'll see.

KITTY. Will they?

JUNE *shakes her head, cheerfully philosophical.*

JUNE. Still. That's as it should be. You're a mother. That's the job.

I'm getting an aspirin. See if I can't take the edge off this tooth thing.

KITTY *nods.* JUNE *starts heading off . . .*

You loved that doll.

A last look back.

You never put it down.

And JUNE*'s gone.* KITTY *examines the doll. A screw in* KITTY*'s head winds that bit tighter. After a while, she suddenly pulls off one of the doll's legs, throws it hard aside. Then the other leg too. It's satisfying work.* KITTY *finds herself in:*

Scene Ten

KITTY*'s kitchen.* KITTY *takes off the dressing gown. Wipes her hands on the apron she wears underneath. She opens a pot of jam, starts daubing it onto the doll. There's a cake on the side.*

CARL (*offstage, calling*). Kitty . . . ?

KITTY. Come through . . .

CARL *appears, struggling with a huge package.*

CARL. You shouldn't leave the door on the latch. I could have been anyone.

KITTY. I could have been anyone once, but it's too late now.

He puts down the package, sees what she's doing . . .

CARL. Oh my God. You're rubbing apricot jam on the breasts of Amputee Barbie?

KITTY. She's Sindy not Barbie. Like Barbie but cheaper.

CARL. I guess that's why she's not putting up much of a fight. Where are her legs?

KITTY. I snapped them off earlier – the work of a moment.

CARL. You could get a webcam and make a fortune doing whatever this is.

KITTY. She's the bride. I stick her on the top of that . . .

CARL. What is that?

KITTY. It's an eight-egg Madeira cooked in a pudding bowl. For the skirt of the wedding dress. I'm making a fondant icing train studded with silver sprinkles and she's carrying a little sugar flower bouquet. I make a veil out of a doily, then I pipe 'Happy Birthday Cora' in pink round the bottom, and there's a candle in the shape of a six over here.

CARL (*amazed*). If only you could use these powers for good instead of evil . . .

KITTY. It's what she wanted. I tried to sell her a mermaid or a princess, but she wanted a bride. She's desperate for Johnny and me to get married.

CARL. You are married.

KITTY. Again – and this time, the works: big meringue dress – that's just for her, then pink doves released from a basket, and heart-shaped pots of bubbles instead of confetti, she says.

CARL. Sounds great – I'm in.

KITTY. I don't know where it comes from. We tried so hard to raise her without any gender stereotyping. Then I went into her room on the morning of her second birthday and found

I'd spawned Ivana fucking Trump. Did you bring the extra icing sugar?

CARL. Oh – yes . . .

He produces it.

KITTY. Great. Drink?

CARL. Are you having one?

KITTY. I am if you make it. Shit, she's such a freakish shape, even marzipan won't mould to her . . .

CARL. Gin?

CARL sets about making drinks.

KITTY. I'm guessing Toni's a no-show?

CARL. I'm sorry – it's his loss.

KITTY. He doesn't like us.

CARL. It's not that. I told you he might have a thing. Do you have any lime?

KITTY. No. I have seventy-two cocktail sausages, twice my bodyweight in cheesy Wotsits, a shedload of cherry tomatoes and a car boot full of mini-chocolate brownies.

CARL. Just ice, then.

KITTY. So, with Toni, is it because we're too old or too straight or there's nowhere to sit that hasn't got a bit of fruit winder stuck on it?

CARL. It's none of those things.

KITTY. Is it Johnny's obsession with the abuse of the apostrophe?

CARL shakes his head.

Is it because Cora once told him she'd done a poo in the shape of a dolphin?

CARL. No, he liked that.

KITTY. Is it Miles?

CARL. No.

KITTY. Because I'd really understand. I mean, I can hardly bear coming here myself these days and it's my home.

CARL. It's not Miles.

KITTY. Well it must be something . . .

CARL (*shrugs, matter-of-fact*). He's just not my boyfriend any more.

KITTY *is astonished, reels*.

KITTY. Since when . . . ?

CARL. A couple of months.

Maybe four.

KITTY (*aghast*). You didn't tell me . . . ?

CARL. I wanted to handle it.

KITTY. You didn't *tell* me?

CARL. I felt . . . stupid.

KITTY. He just answered the phone, when I called about bringing the icing sugar . . .

CARL (*shrugs*). He's still living with me.

KITTY *fixes him with a look*.

KITTY. Carl . . .

CARL. It works out well.

KITTY. No.

CARL. Okay – stop it, I know what you're thinking.

KITTY. No you don't.

CARL. And it's insulting.

KITTY (*a confession*). Yes it is.

CARL. He's not . . . exploiting me. It's just a reality – he's got no money, Kitty. Where can he go?

KITTY. Back where he came from.

CARL. Salonika?

KITTY. Oh, shit. I hate this.

CARL. Well me too! For God's sake, I introduced him to people at work – I've never done anything like that before. I've been carrying on like a lovestruck teenager. Made an absolute berk of myself.

It was great.

KITTY. So what went wrong?

CARL (*shrugs*). I put coasters under his drinks sometimes. He didn't like it. I think I'm too old a dog for new tricks.

KITTY. You're not old – you're my age.

CARL. It's more in gay years.

KITTY. Well I wish you'd told me . . .

CARL. I just wanted it to last a bit longer. You know, the *feeling*. It was so . . . amazing at the start . . . I mean, how are you meant to know that'll change?

KITTY. Aside from past experience?

CARL. But I thought about you and Johnny . . .

KITTY. What about us?

CARL. How you met and everything.

KITTY. That party?

CARL. The way he described it: he said he walked in and everyone else seemed grey – and there you were across the room: like a firework.

KITTY (*remembering*). But I wasn't a firework. I was in flames.

CARL. He put you out. You dropped and rolled together.

KITTY. Yeah.

CARL. And you're together still.

KITTY. Just about.

CARL. No, no. You're together. It's possible. The passion and the permanence. I don't know. It just felt so right with Toni – so *happy*. But then . . .

Maybe it was the moon.

He shrugs.

KITTY. Oh Carl . . .

CARL. You know when I was a kid, my dad used to tell me when a full moon was due. He had to notify his whole station watch to expect trouble. Can you believe they used to warn the police when the full moon came around . . . ? Maybe they still do.

Maybe that was all it was.

Noise offstage.

Oh – don't say anything – not tonight. I'm over the worst of it and I can't stand the idea of two straight men trying to commiserate.

KITTY *nods, looks up –* MILES *and* JOHNNY *have appeared,* JOHNNY *carrying packages.*

KITTY. Oh – hi – did you get the . . .

JOHNNY. Piñata!

JOHNNY *reveals a papier mâché donkey.*

KITTY. Balloons.

JOHNNY. No.

KITTY. Why not?

MILES. Carlito!

He falls on CARL, *embraces him with excess warmth.*

CARL. How are you?

KITTY. The guy said they were ready . . .

MILES. Never better . . .

JOHNNY. We got there too late.

MILES. Kitty, I'm sorry, the balloon thing, all my fault. Just had a *fabulous* meeting – which overran.

JOHNNY. I'm sorry.

KITTY *fights to be nice. It's a massive effort.*

KITTY. Miles is AA now.

MILES. It was that or the boot from the firm. My secretary, Susie, drops me there, and Johnny picks me up – makes sure I'm not bunking off.

JOHNNY. It's on my way home . . . I work late on a Wednesday.

KITTY. Johnny facilitates an interfaith support group after school on a Wednesday. Another step in his bid to become the teacher with the longest hours in the country.

CARL. 'Interfaith support'?

JOHNNY. Trying to be positive about what the various faith groups represented in the school have in common.

KITTY. You'll be shocked to learn there's next to nothing.

CARL. Anal sex?

MILES. No thanks.

CARL. They're all against it, I was thinking.

JOHNNY. That's depressingly true. Miles – diet Coke?

JOHNNY *starts making drinks.* KITTY *corners him.*

KITTY. So . . . ?

JOHNNY. Look, I'll get them tomorrow.

KITTY. Tomorrow's too late. It's her birthday tomorrow.

CARL. So, things are going okay for you, Miles . . . ?

MILES. Met the *best* bunch of people at AA.

CARL. Uh-huh.

JOHNNY. They'll be here for the party.

KITTY. But not when she wakes up . . .

MILES. An actor off one of those hospital shows *and* a real doctor – funny.

KITTY. I ordered the damn things. You just had to get there in time to collect them.

JOHNNY. *Big* picture, Kit, yeah?

KITTY *seethes, as* JOHNNY *hands* MILES *his drink.*

MILES. I wish I'd known them back when we were all still drinking – could've had a blast!

KITTY *rededicates herself to the cake.*

CARL. Right.

MILES. And I'm looking for a flat, of course.

JOHNNY (*for* KITTY*'s benefit*). Yeah, it's taking a little while.

KITTY (*barely engaging*). The Ice Age took 'a little while'.

MILES (*to* CARL). They're being fantastic about it. But it's got to be somewhere the kids can come, feel at home. I've just not seen the right gaff yet.

CARL. So you're thinking the split's maybe permanent?

MILES (*sighing*). We went to the zoo last weekend, Carl. Bea'd been wanting to do it since you talked about it and we try to do something all together every now and then for Het and Tommy's sake. So we went and we looked at the bears' enclosure. We waited for ever – not a sniff – but then all of a sudden, this slightly manky-looking beast appeared.

And it was doing this thing with its head, this side-to-side thing. And I'd seen a sign earlier saying one of the bears had this distressed routine because she'd been kept in too small a cage at another zoo, but they were hoping she'd improve with time and the right kind of care, you know . . .

So I watched this poor ungainly thing . . . side to side . . . side to side . . .

(*He darkens*.). . . . and then Tommy touched my arm – he said: 'Dad?' . . .

. . . he said 'Dad?' . . .

And my face was all wet. Just streaming with . . . wet . . . just falling down my face . . . everyone watching.

So . . .

I think pretty permanent.

CARL. Right.

A terrible silence.

JOHNNY. You'll be okay, Miles.

MILES. Course I will.

(*Rallying*.) I tell you, Carl, you get into trouble – these are the guys you want in your corner.

CARL. I'm sure that's right.

JOHNNY *eyes* CARL'*s present, determined to change the mood*.

JOHNNY. Carl – huge package!

CARL *takes a moment to adjust* . . .

CARL. Oh – yes . . . the Little Miss Deluxe.

MILES. Is that an inflatable?

KITTY *flinches, says nothing*.

CARL. It's a karaoke machine with this special mat that you dance on to operate the disco lights.

MILES. Wow!

JOHNNY. She'll go berserk.

JOHNNY *picks up his own packages*.

D'you want to bring it through . . . ? Put it with the other stuff . . . ?

CARL. Oh – sure . . .

JOHNNY and CARL go.

MILES. Quite a thing, this party.

KITTY. Yeah.

MILES. Bea always hired somewhere, never did it at home.

KITTY. She had the right idea.

MILES. No – it was all . . . bought cake, paid entertainer. And it wasn't as if she was working! I mean, she couldn't possibly have done *that*.

He nods towards the cake.

KITTY. The guilt of the working mother manifests itself in mysterious ways.

MILES. No! God, look at you, Kitty. You can do *anything*.

KITTY. It's just a cake, Miles.

MILES. I should've married someone more like you.

KITTY. What . . . !?

MILES. It's true. Someone strong-minded. But I didn't have the guts. I was too stupid back then, when I was younger. Scared. I'd never've dared to ask *you* out.

KITTY. That's good cos I'd've said no.

MILES. Would you?

KITTY. I should think so.

MILES. You were choosy?

KITTY. I chose Johnny.

KITTY flashes a warning look at MILES. A momentary flicker of something between them.

MILES (*resuming*). See – you know your own mind. Bea's not like that.

KITTY. Well it takes all sorts.

MILES. Oh Kit, you've no idea. She's this endlessly hungry permanently empty thing. She gorges herself on the most awful crap – you should see what she reads – it's obscene, but . . . nothing fills her up.

KITTY. What kind of crap?

MILES. All these magazines women read that give them ludicrous expectations of themselves.

KITTY. Don't men read magazines too?

MILES. Yes, that give them ludicrous expectations of women. Not just magazines either, these awful books – you know – *Women Who Love Too Much*. I mean, have *you* read that?

KITTY. No.

MILES. Course you haven't. *Women Who Love Too Much*. I had a look through it – absolute bollocks.

KITTY. Well what were you expecting?

MILES. With a title like that, a couple of phone numbers would've been nice . . .

MILES *considers a moment*.

You know the only book she's read in years that wasn't a self-help tome or the Boden catalogue? That one you told her about.

KITTY. Which one?

MILES. Bloody depressing actually.

KITTY. Which book?

MILES. The sex life of someone. French woman.

KITTY. *La Vie Sexuelle* – it's not 'sex life', it's 'sexual life'.

MILES. Is there a big difference?

KITTY. I think probably yes.

MILES. You make me feel a blunt instrument, Kitty.

> JOHNNY *and* CARL *come back in.*

KITTY. So, did Bea like it?

MILES. I think she liked the *idea* of reading it better than the experience.

KITTY. And you found it depressing.

JOHNNY. Found what depressing?

MILES. The sexual life of a French woman.

JOHNNY. Oh.

CARL. Any one in particular?

KITTY. She's a very highly respected academic.

MILES. With a penchant for group sex. Her and a load of blokes preferably.

JOHNNY. This rings a dim bell.

MILES. I thought there was something sad about it. Kitty recommended it to Bea . . .

KITTY. I didn't.

MILES. Inspired her then, one night at dinner. You said you'd found it liberating. Don't you remember this, Johnny?

JOHNNY. You'd think I would . . . I can tell I ought to . . .

KITTY (*getting irritated*). You know I didn't recommend the book . . . and I didn't find it *sexually* liberating . . . I just found it a relief to be in the head of someone who instead of being trained to consider the world one great sexual threat saw one giant sexual prospect. That mindset – I found that refreshing, a relief, that's all. Is that so frigging weird?

> KITTY *rededicates herself to the cake.*

MILES. It's a queer sort of fantasy. All those blokes.

CARL. I'll name that tune in one.

JOHNNY. Well surely the point is it's a *female* fantasy.

KITTY *doesn't even look up*.

KITTY. It's not a fantasy, it's how she lives her life.

MILES. John's right – it's 'What if a woman thought like a bloke?', you know. Took on all comers. As it were.

JOHNNY. Which is not to say all blokes think like that.

KITTY *struggles to screen out the conversation*.

MILES. Well, I would say, for the most part, *straight* blokes, at least, divide women into three categories –

JOHNNY *and* CARL *smile at one another* – MILES *is off again* . . .

– the ones they'd give anything to sleep with, the ones they'd sleep with if they were pissed . . .

That's enough – KITTY *makes quietly for the door*.

CARL. And their mothers.

MILES. No! – the ones they'd sleep with if they were pissed as long as no one else ever found out.

JOHNNY *laughs*.

JOHNNY. Oh, for God's sake . . .

MILES. I'm sorry, Kitty, but if it's any consolation, you'd absolutely be in the first category.

The laughter peters out. They realise KITTY*'s gone*.

CARL. Oh . . .

Half an understanding of something.

JOHNNY. You guys go through, I'll . . .

CARL. Sure . . .

CARL *leads* MILES *away, leaving* JOHNNY *alone*. KITTY *enters the space, fights off her apron, throws it on the floor*. JOHNNY *turns, sees her. After a moment:*

JOHNNY. What're you doing?

KITTY *breathes*.

KITTY. I'm wondering at what point it became acceptable for you to stand in this house on which I pay the mortgage, drinking the drinks I bought out of the glasses I washed in front of the cake I baked and talk that fucking talk. All – and I think this is a lovely touch for which I must take full credit – while I'm wearing an apron.

JOHNNY (*smiling, antagonistic*). Oh God, here it comes . . .

KITTY. Here it comes.

JOHNNY. We got a bit boys-y.

KITTY. Yeah, I guess you used up all your political correctness at school this week.

JOHNNY. Okay – this is actually about the balloons, right?

KITTY *scoffs, hostile*.

Oh – wait – I might have left the freezer door open in 1993?

KITTY *turns on him*.

KITTY (*angry, serious*). You don't get it, do you . . . ?

JOHNNY. I get that Miles is a pressure . . . I'm not completely stupid. But he'll be gone soon.

KITTY. Oh, will he?

JOHNNY. He's looking at places all the time.

KITTY. Is he?

JOHNNY. Of course he is.

KITTY. Drinking, fucking and lying, John? You don't think he's given up all three? Christ – you're so naïve.

JOHNNY. I'm not fashionably cynical, if that's what you mean!

KITTY (*'as'* JOHNNY). 'Oh, Miles, you look so well.' (*'As'* MILES.) 'Looked out of the window once last week, caught a bit of sun . . . ' . . . Haven't you noticed the orange tidemark in the bathroom sink?

JOHNNY *fails to make the link.*

JOHNNY. What?

KITTY. It's fake tan, you twat! It's a paint job! Why do you think we're having to boil wash all the towels?

JOHNNY *baffles, but then it starts to make sense . . .*

Oh – hang on – you don't do the laundry.

JOHNNY. A fake tan . . .

KITTY. Ya-hah.

JOHNNY. But . . . ? That's absurd . . . Why would Miles . . . ?

KITTY (*laughs*). You're blind as a bat, John. You can't see a hand in front of you. You can't see how bad things are. You can't see what's coming!

KITTY *stops laughing, the energy drained out of her.*

You can't see what's coming . . .

JOHNNY *looks forlorn.*

God . . .

JOHNNY. Okay, so maybe it's not just about Miles.

KITTY *breathes a moment.*

KITTY. You know . . . when I got to the hospital after my dad's thing blew . . . he'd been technically dead and they'd brought him back to life, but the doctors said it was still in the balance . . .

JOHNNY. I know . . .

KITTY. And what I thought was . . . I thought:

'Oh, shit . . . don't let him die – not my dad, don't let my dad die!' Because I need to ask him this one thing:

Was it after I left home he suddenly realised he didn't want to be part of our family any more? Or had he just been waiting to leave, barely clinging on for years? Going through the motions every day . . . ? How long had he been waiting?

The phone begins to ring in the background.

Something bad's coming, John.

JOHNNY *hears this*.

JOHNNY. No it's not. Not if we don't want it to.

KITTY. I'm telling you now, something bad . . .

JOHNNY (*cuts her off*). Okay – I accept things have been hard lately, and I'm sure I played a part in that, but . . . nothing bad is coming unless we let it, and this . . .

He gestures towards her.

. . . thing you're doing is just . . . crap . . .

The phone stops.

This is just talking for effect!

But KITTY *shakes her head, sad, serious.*

Kitty . . .

KITTY. It's fucked, John.

JOHNNY. Don't say that.

KITTY. We're fucked.

CARL *appears, anxious. He has the phone. After a moment.*

JOHNNY. Yeah, what is it, Carl?

CARL. I'm sorry . . . it's for Kitty.

He holds out the phone.

KITTY. What is it, Carl?

He shrugs, sorry, a proper warning.

CARL. It's Something Bad.

Scene Eleven

Hotel bar, the aftermath of a funeral. Muzak plays. Voices rise and fall, slightly hushed.

MICHAEL, *alone, sips a drink.*

KITTY *watches a second, takes a deep breath, approaches.*

MICHAEL. Nicely judged.

KITTY. Thank you.

MICHAEL. It was.

KITTY. The least I could do, in the circs . . .

MICHAEL *nods.*

MICHAEL. I like the way you didn't make the end seem like a defeat. It's always hard, that. I mean, it is a defeat of course, however it happens. It's a fucking fiasco. But you finessed that very nicely . . .

KITTY. I wanted to be clear that Stephanie had taken control, at the end. Without getting into the suicide.

MICHAEL. I wasn't so sure about 'Seasons in the Sun'.

KITTY. No, me neither. The parents' call.

MICHAEL. Ah.

Beat.

KITTY. I'm surprised you're here in person. Most organisations just sent flowers.

MICHAEL *looks at* KITTY *a moment.*

MICHAEL. I've always found funerals a good place to pick up women. They get a bit teary, then it's *carpe diem*, a Malibu Glide, and Bob's your uncle.

KITTY. That's possibly a joke.

MICHAEL. It possibly is: I've tied in seeing the regional office tomorrow – a beard for my hideous disfiguring compassion.

KITTY. Staying here?

MICHAEL *nods*.

MICHAEL. Seems alright. You?

KITTY. Driving home.

MICHAEL. No drink then.

KITTY. The obligatory cream sherry of remembrance.

MICHAEL. Not the cheap blended whisky of regret?

KITTY. I'm a woman, I wasn't offered a whisky.

MICHAEL. Ah.

He smiles. KITTY *takes him in. Then she breaks away.*

KITTY. Well . . . I ought to . . .

MICHAEL. Nice to see you again. Gave me something pleasant
to latch onto in the gloom.

KITTY stops, irked, mocks him.

Oh . . . Too modest. Or too cynical.

KITTY. No – it's just – the last time our paths crossed, you
barely recognised me.

MICHAEL. What?

KITTY. So I take the compliments with a pinch of salt.

MICHAEL. You mean the euthanasia seminar?

KITTY smirks.

(*Indignant.*) I recognised you!

KITTY. Really.

MICHAEL. I didn't make a *move* on you, if that's what you're
. . . Oh, don't tell me that's what you expected? At a
euthanasia seminar?

KITTY is wrongfooted.

KITTY. I wouldn't have thought it was beyond you . . .

MICHAEL. But I didn't – so you were . . . insulted . . . ?

KITTY. I wasn't insulted!

KITTY *steadies herself, remembers where she is.*

I just thought, given your behaviour the first time we met, it would have been an idea to acknowledge one another in a manner that smoothed the way for a debate about living wills and endstage exit strategies.

MICHAEL. Okay – two things you need to know: One – I am a stickler for professional etiquette and I would never put you in a position where you felt uncomfortable at work. Two – I never fuck around on home turf.

KITTY. Oh, could you say that again a bit louder . . . I don't think Aunt Elsie quite caught it . . .

MICHAEL (*pressing on, irritated*). When I'm away, by all means, but at home, no . . . No! It would be disrespectful, an insult to my wife.

KITTY. I wonder if she knows how lucky she is?

MICHAEL. Don't patronise my wife – you don't know her. She's not what you think.

KITTY. Really – well enlighten me . . . does she do it too? Put herself about a bit . . . ?

MICHAEL. No. Least I don't think so.

KITTY. So it would bother you?

MICHAEL. If I knew, probably.

KITTY. She probably does it.

MICHAEL. She probably doesn't.

KITTY. What's to stop her?

MICHAEL. Opportunity. She has an immensely busy job.

KITTY. So do I.

MICHAEL. And you don't do it, do you?

KITTY. I don't do it with *you*!

MICHAEL *smiles*.

MICHAEL. Now we're getting somewhere.

KITTY *pulls back – reins it in*.

KITTY. Thank you for coming. I know the family appreciates it.

MICHAEL. Drive safely.

KITTY. I will.

MICHAEL (*as* KITTY *turns away*). No really. You look tired.

KITTY *looks back at him for a moment, surprised. It's been a while since anyone noticed*.

KITTY. I am.

KITTY *stands in his gaze for a moment, confused, then takes herself off to a far corner, collects a second cream sherry. MICHAEL wanders over to a different corner. KITTY watches discreetly as MICHAEL drains his Scotch*.

JOHNNY'S VOICE. 'Long, long ago in a far away place . . . '

MILES *enters* BEA's *garden, collapses. Stays where he's fallen*.

In the hotel bar, KITTY *swaps her empty sherry glass for a full one*.

At KITTY *and* JOHNNY's, CARL *hurries in, taking off his coat, closely followed by* JOHNNY, *pulling his on*.

CARL. It's no problem . . .

JOHNNY *seems sad, beleaguered*.

JOHNNY. I just couldn't think who else to ask – Cora's been having these nightmares lately. I think it's partly the atmosphere here . . . things have been . . .

Not good.

CARL. I know . . . It's a phase.

JOHNNY (*unconvinced*). I hope so.

> Plus – they did 'stranger danger' at school and it scared the pants off her. So Kitty tried to put things in perspective . . . told her you're much more likely to be harmed by someone you know, or a member of your own family . . .

CARL. That must've helped.

JOHNNY. Exactly. I just thought, if she wakes up it's got to be someone she really feels comfortable with. Tim sleeps like a log . . .

CARL. It's fine.

JOHNNY. And you came with a balloon and everything!

CARL. Oh – Toni left it. It's my goodbye present.

JOHNNY. Goodbye?

CARL. He left this morning.

JOHNNY. For Salonika?

CARL. Kentish Town. He thought this would cheer me up.

> JOHNNY *absorbs this*.

JOHNNY. Has it?

> CARL *shrugs*.

> I'm so sorry.

CARL. It's fine. A relief really. Having him around made it hard bringing other people home, you know?

> JOHNNY *baffles*.

JOHNNY. Right. Yes, it would.

> Well, I shouldn't be long . . .

> (*Checks for the car keys*.) Apparently Miles just turned up, drunk, wanting to tell the kids about this flat he found . . . Bea wouldn't let him in, so he got a bit difficult . . .

CARL. But he's asleep now . . . ?

JOHNNY. In the garden. She's calling the police if I don't . . .

CARL. Go – go get him.

JOHNNY. You're a friend, Carl. To me and Kitty both, I mean.
And I'm sorry about . . .

CARL. Go on . . .

*CARL hurries JOHNNY offstage, watches after him a
moment, then exhales. Looks up at the balloon.*

*At the hotel, KITTY watches as MICHAEL takes off his
jacket, undoes his tie. He looks drained, hangs his clothes on
a hook, transforming his space into the hotel room.*

*At KITTY's house, CARL looks out front, out of the window
into the night, ominous.*

Look at that moon . . .

CARL goes off, takes his balloon.

*KITTY watches as MICHAEL unbuttons his shirt, takes it
off, unself-conscious. Then his shoes and his trousers.
MICHAEL looks at himself in a mirror. He assesses the view
face on, then sideways, sucks in his gut, lets it go again. Hah
– relief. He pulls on a white towelling robe.*

KITTY picks up another sherry.

*MICHAEL sits down, stares straight ahead. KITTY watches,
drains her sherry glass. Her head is swimming now.*

*A door buzzer sounds in MICHAEL's room. He looks up, sur-
prised. KITTY steps into the space, waits. MICHAEL steps
up to meet her . . . a beat, before:*

KITTY. What's a Malibu Glide?

MICHAEL. It's . . . a sugary drink.

She considers a moment.

KITTY. Let's skip that bit, then . . .

She steps forward, kisses MICHAEL . . . *He responds but* KITTY*'s advances become much more aggressive . . .*

MICHAEL. Hey . . .

She goes to kiss him again.

Stop . . .

KITTY. Why?

She's on him again now, he has to push her firmly away, hold her at arms' length.

MICHAEL. No!

KITTY. What . . . ?

MICHAEL. I don't want to.

KITTY. Yes you do.

MICHAEL. No I don't.

KITTY *pulls back, takes him in.*

KITTY. Oh my God – you're rejecting me . . .

MICHAEL. No I'm not . . .

KITTY. You're turning me down . . .

MICHAEL. You're upset.

KITTY. Cheer me up.

MICHAEL. No – you're drunk.

KITTY. Can you not take advantage of that?

She lunges towards him again. He pulls back.

MICHAEL. Your tongue tastes like out-of-date Tiramisu . . .

KITTY. I thought you were indiscriminate!

MICHAEL. I am but I'm not unkind!

He has to push her off – hard.

KITTY. Shit!

KITTY *steadies herself, astonished . . . gradually seems to accept defeat, collect herself a little, moves behind* MICHAEL *to pick up a cushion from the chair. She centres herself, then turns and swings it very hard at* MICHAEL*'s head.*

MICHAEL. Bloody . . .

The cushion connects, flies out of KITTY*'s hands with the force of the blow. She stands defiant as* MICHAEL *recovers, looks pretty humourless. He slowly crosses to pick up the cushion. He carefully replumps it. The image of restraint and maturity.*

Then he whacks KITTY *hard in the head with it.*

KITTY *reels, steadies herself.* MICHAEL*'s still holding his cushion, raising it, threatening in self-defence. There's no trace of a smile.*

KITTY *dodges and feints, works him round till she's close enough to the chair to get the other cushion, goes on the attack.*

They're relatively well-matched, MICHAEL*'s strength balanced by* KITTY*'s speed. It's a long ugly brawl, increasing in violence until an exhausted* MICHAEL *finally manages to pin down a winded* KITTY.

He has her trapped, sits astride her ribs, holds the cushion up, ominous, over her face.

KITTY. Go on – do it . . . I dare you! Go on!

He hesitates, tempted, still full of adrenalin, then subsides, throws the cushion aside, clambers off her, crawls a little way away and lies recovering.

After a while:

MICHAEL. You fucking freak.

KITTY *starts to laugh. Finally* MICHAEL *joins in.*

KITTY. I'm sorry.

MICHAEL. Forget it. I've had worse.

KITTY. Really?

He collects himself. Gets up, pours a glass of whisky for himself, water for KITTY, *presses it on her. She drinks, sitting up slightly.* MICHAEL *collapses in the chair, catches his breath.*

Oh – my top . . .

MICHAEL *looks.*

MICHAEL. You've lost a button.

KITTY. Well don't gawp . . .

MICHAEL breathes – this woman's annoying. KITTY *tries to hold the front of her shirt closed, absurdly prim.*

MICHAEL. Hang on. There's a sewing kit thing in the . . .

He goes off to the bathroom. KITTY *lies back down, exhausted, drunk.* MICHAEL *comes back with a pin.*

Here . . . safety pin.

KITTY. I'll do it.

MICHAEL. Be my guest.

He sits down again.

KITTY. Ow!

KITTY*'s pricked herself.*

MICHAEL. Christ.

KITTY. My finger – I pricked it . . .

She holds it out, plaintive. MICHAEL *can hardly find the strength.*

MICHAEL. Loo roll.

He gets up, goes off again. KITTY *curls up, sorry for herself.* MICHAEL *comes back in.*

Here . . .

But KITTY *doesn't move.*

Here . . . Kitty kitty kitty . . . ?

She's asleep. MICHAEL *sits back down. Peace at last.*

(*After a while.*) Yes, I've had worse.

(*He recalls.*) This Calvinist once who needed spanking to get herself going, then suddenly looked all glum. I asked her what was wrong? She said: 'I'm just thinking how lonely and depressed I'll feel afterwards.'

He shakes his head, confides in KITTY *who still sleeps soundly.*

I found that demoralising.

He settles back into solitude. KITTY *sleeps on.*

JOHNNY *arrives in* BEA's *garden, finds* MILES, *hurries over.*

JOHNNY. Miles . . . ? Miles . . .

He bends over MILES, *rolls him slightly.* BEA *looks out at them.*

Oh look at you . . .

MILES. Bloody cold, John.

JOHNNY. We'll get you inside, Miles.

MILES. Bloody cold out here. Cold outside, Johnny.

JOHNNY. I know, I know.

MILES. Bloody cold.

JOHNNY. Up you come. We'll get you up, Miles . . .

JOHNNY *tries to lift* MILES, *but he's a dead weight – it's incredibly hard.*

MILES. Don't bother. I'm alright.

JOHNNY. No. Get up.

JOHNNY *tries again.*

(*Beginning to get upset.*) Get up.

Now MILES *manages to unbalance* JOHNNY *and tip him to the ground.*

MILES. Oh! Dragged y'down t'my level. Mm . . . ? Finally.

JOHNNY *breathes, the impossibility of lifting* MILES *dawning now.*

They sit like that a while.

God, I'm an ugly nasty fuck, aren't I, Johnny . . . ? Ugly nasty fuck.

JOHNNY. Stop. No.

JOHNNY *tries to embrace* MILES. MILES *starts to laugh.*

MILES. Oh, you've got to laugh.

He laughs more until he starts to cry. JOHNNY *holds him.* MILES *laughs/cries on, rocking, distraught, in* JOHNNY*'s arms.*

You've got to laugh.

JOHNNY. Don't laugh.

JOHNNY *holds him hard.*

Don't laugh.

JOHNNY *rocks him.*

Don't laugh. I think you're beautiful.

MILES*' tears subside, he dozes in* JOHNNY*'s arms.*

After a while:

MILES. Oh, I'm tired, Johnny. Need to sleep. Sleep for a hundred years. Have some lovely dreams then, hm?

JOHNNY. Yeah, what'll you dream of, Miles . . . ?

MILES. Same things as everyone else, John. Pretty wife. Lovely kids . . .

JOHNNY. Yeah . . .

MILES *falls asleep in* JOHNNY*'s arms.*

Yeah.

BEA *disappears.* JOHNNY *gathers his strength, manages to drag* MILES *up off the ground, get him away, leaving* KITTY *and* MICHAEL *alone on stage.*

KITTY *suddenly sits up, confused. Her shirt is still open.*

KITTY. Have we had sex?

MICHAEL. It wasn't memorable.

KITTY. We've not, have we? Have we?

MICHAEL. Wouldn't you know?

KITTY. I don't know. I feel . . .

She doesn't know. Bruised maybe.

How long have I been asleep?

MICHAEL. A couple of hours.

KITTY. God.

She looks at him again, suspicious.

MICHAEL. We've not had sex! F'goodness' sake!

KITTY *relaxes . . . accepts this now. Still:*

KITTY. Well it happens. It's on the increase. Men shagging women when they're . . .

MICHAEL. So I hear. It's not my thing.

KITTY. It's what happened to Sleeping Beauty.

MICHAEL. Excuse me?

KITTY *explains, battling her exhaustion, gradually recovering.*

KITTY. Sleeping Beauty. In the old Italian version, before the Victorians changed it, the spell gets cast and they burn all the spindles, and Sleeping Beauty's forbidden to go near any needles and all that . . .

And she doesn't. She's a good girl, she stays away. But one day she's outside, exploring, and she gets a splinter of flax stuck in her finger.

MICHAEL. A splinter of flax?

KITTY. And she falls asleep. Then, years later, she's still asleep, a prince comes along, but he doesn't wake her with a kiss. He just thinks – oh, excellent, checks there's no one around and fucks her.

MICHAEL. Good lord.

KITTY. She's in this kind of coma and he fucks her and rides off – and she still doesn't wake up. But she's pregnant now.

MICHAEL. You're kidding . . . ?

KITTY. No – with twins. And she gives birth to them . . .

MICHAEL. She's still asleep?

KITTY. And after they're born the babies crawl over the body looking for food, looking for the nipple. And one makes it, but the other can't find the way, sucks on her finger by accident –

MICHAEL. Sucks out the splinter of flax . . . ?

KITTY. Exactly. So she wakes. Her children wake her.

MICHAEL *absorbs the new world order.*

MICHAEL. How d'you know that?

KITTY. I looked it up. I have to read the official version to my daughter all the time, and it never made sense, so I looked it up.

MICHAEL. God.

KITTY *struggles to her feet, goes to pour water.*

KITTY. I know. Nothing's innocent, is it?

MICHAEL. I don't set much store by innocence.

KITTY. Why am I not surprised?

KITTY *drinks a glass down.*

MICHAEL. It makes me nervous, innocence, it's too easily abused. That's why you've got to hold the line in favour of *experience*. Make a fetish of innocence and before y'know it, we'll be overrun by an army of abstinence perverts.

KITTY. Is that likely?

MICHAEL. I saw this kid on TV the other week – a Silver Ring Thinger, he was – the ones who're going to *wait*. Fourteen maybe. He was warning others kids to beware oral sex because it was addictive . . . 'Once you pop,' he said, 'you can't stop.'

(*Shakes his head, aghast.*) What have they done to these children that they can't tell the difference between a pussy and a Pringle! I tell you, if my son came home with a 'silver ring', I'd pull it off his finger, melt it down into a bullet, buy a gun and shoot myself between the eyes with it – because I'd know I'd failed utterly.

KITTY. Maybe you'd feel differently if you had a daughter . . .

MICHAEL. I hope not. Cos then they'd really have won, wouldn't they? The Silver Ringers and the Pope and the Mullahs and the skinheads and all the other people whose worst nightmare *you* are.

KITTY *absorbs this.*

KITTY. So you're not just a lecherous git, you're Fucking For Freedom?

MICHAEL. Yes. The FFF. Join us, why don't you.

KITTY. I just tried and had my application rejected.

MICHAEL. Try again. You seem on a more even keel. We might smile on you second time around.

Beat.

You're not going to.

KITTY. No.

MICHAEL. Which is interesting. Because you want to.

    KITTY *smiles*.

What then?

KITTY. No . . .

MICHAEL. Come on – I can take it . . .

    KITTY *considers a moment. A fresh realisation:*

KITTY. The truth?

MICHAEL. If you can't tell the truth in a hotel room, God help us.

KITTY. Because it wasn't my idea.

    MICHAEL *hears this – it's unexpected.*

MICHAEL. That's it?

KITTY (*nods*). I need it to be my idea.

MICHAEL. I see . . .

    KITTY *shrugs – 'sorry' – but* MICHAEL *smiles.*

No – I like that . . . I especially like the way it implies that it might be, one day . . . ?

    KITTY *smiles.*

KITTY. You might not want me.

MICHAEL. I will want you.

    MICHAEL *looks at her, begins to laugh.*

Yes, I like it. I like it.

    KITTY *pulls on her jacket, getting ready to leave. But something holds her back.*

KITTY. Well. Goodbye, Stephanie.

    MICHAEL *reflects a moment.*

MICHAEL. Goodbye, Stephanie.

KITTY. It makes you think.

MICHAEL. For sure.

MICHAEL nods.

KITTY. My husband's delightful.

MICHAEL. I should hope so.

KITTY. For the most part. And the kids, they're . . .

She shrugs: 'They're just great.'

MICHAEL. Well then. What more could you want?

KITTY considers the question for a second.

KITTY. I want to be happy.

MICHAEL absorbs this, smiles.

MICHAEL. Kitty – your wish is granted!

KITTY laughs.

I mean it.

KITTY. You can't do that.

He picks up his Scotch, hands KITTY her water.

MICHAEL. Why not? I can. Here. I give you permission to be happy. Take it, Kitty. Take it.

They raise their drinks. He holds her gaze, something is transacted between them. Then they clink glasses, drink, still bound up in one another.

A beat.

Do you know why we clink glasses . . . ? Because all the other senses are catered for . . .

KITTY registers this, smiles . . . MICHAEL leans forward and they begin to kiss . . . it becomes a deep, involved, fabulous kiss . . . That goes on. And on. Until . . . perhaps inevitably . . .

They part.

MICHAEL absorbs this, philosophical. KITTY collects herself – with some effort. She's going to leave.

KITTY. Well. I'll see you at the next . . .

MICHAEL. You'll see me, I'm around.

> *She waits a moment, half-apologetic.* MICHAEL *smiles.*

Go home and fuck your husband then.

> MICHAEL *wanders off with his drink, leaving* KITTY *alone.*

Scene Twelve

KITTY *finds herself – at home.* JOHNNY *comes to meet her, in his dressing gown. He's relieved to see her.*

JOHNNY. You're late.

KITTY. Yeah.

JOHNNY. I was worried.

KITTY. Yeah.

JOHNNY. I thought you might not, you know . . . come back.

KITTY. Me too.

JOHNNY. Miles is still here.

KITTY. I'm not surprised.

JOHNNY. And Carl's on the sofa.

KITTY. Oh . . . ?

JOHNNY. He babysat while I went to get Miles . . .

KITTY. Okay.

> *Beat.*

JOHNNY. I want to kiss you, Kitty.

KITTY. Really?

JOHNNY. Badly.

KITTY. Okay.

He holds her, kisses her. KITTY *responds, but only up to a point.* JOHNNY *squeezes and releases her repeatedly, checking she's really there.*

JOHNNY. You taste different.

KITTY. It's sherry.

JOHNNY. I like it. You know you're everything to me.

KITTY. I'm everything to everyone. Sometimes I get excited at the thought of being nothing to someone for twenty minutes.

JOHNNY. I'm a good husband, Kitty. Underneath.

KITTY *smiles, sadly.*

KITTY. That's what my mother says.

Beat.

JOHNNY. Are you coming up?

A moment's hesitation.

KITTY. I'm right behind you . . .

The end of Elgar's 'Salut d'Amour' comes up very quietly . . . JOHNNY smiles as he goes off, looking back a couple of times – happy, relieved to have his wife home.

As soon as he's gone . . .

Scene Thirteen

BEA *appears. We're in her kitchen, it's transformed. The Elgar plays on,* KITTY *still lost in it.* BEA *waits till the melody plays out, ends . . .*

KITTY (*coming to*). Oh – sorry . . .

KITTY *takes off her coat, only now fully entering the scene.*

I was . . . Nice music.

BEA. Carl's Elgar. You know, the 'Salut d'Amour' from the zoo.

KITTY. Ah.

BEA. I don't like it as much as I thought I would. But then I'm not very good with classical music. Wasn't brought up with it. Still.

KITTY. Still.

An awkward moment.

Well look, Bea . . . I actually came because . . .

BEA. You think I ought to take Miles back.

KITTY. No. No, I came because . . . we've been friends a long time.

BEA. You're Miles' friends.

KITTY. Well – this is the point – we're there for you and the kids as well. And you know Miles is . . . much better. He's doing really well getting used to his new place. Gradually. And his drinking's much . . . steadier.

MILES *hurries in, separate space, with a bottle of wine.*

MILES (*calling off*). I'll open the Cab Shiraz ready, Johnny . . .

MILES *turns on the TV, settles in front of it.*

(*Brightening, amazed.*) Hey – there's an advert for the exact same bottle!

MILES *marvels, delighted.*

KITTY. I mean, you could talk to him. If you wanted to. I know things seem impossible sometimes but . . .

BEA. We don't want Miles back, Kitty.

A burst of taped laughter from MILES' *TV.*

KITTY. Oh.

BEA. The thing is, you don't expect to shine when you marry a man like Miles. But you don't expect to become invisible.

KITTY. No.

BEA. So we've started again without him. I feel ten years younger already. Lost almost a stone with the upset, so I'm looking pretty good. And I'm retraining . . .

KITTY. To go back to work . . . ?

BEA. I know – it's a shock. I've not had a job since I was Miles' PA. But I looked at Johnny, how . . . passionate he is about his job. The satisfaction he gets from helping other people. We live such ludicrously insulated lives. I felt I wanted to break out of that, do something that would really make a difference in the world. I felt I had something to offer.

KITTY. You're going into teaching?

BEA. I'm going to be a life coach. I'm doing a course, it starts Monday.

KITTY. Wow . . . How . . . how long does it last . . . ?

BEA. Until Friday.

KITTY *goggles*.

Go on – laugh if you want to.

KITTY. I wasn't.

BEA. I don't mind.

KITTY. Bea . . .

BEA. Anyway, enough about me. How about *you*, Kitty. How've *you* been . . . ?

KITTY*'s suddenly on the back foot*.

KITTY. Oh – good. You know – busy.

BEA. And how's your father these days . . . ?

KITTY. Ha! Lurches from one life-threatening saga to the next, you know . . .

BEA. Has all that brought you closer, do you think . . . ?

> KITTY*'s caught out by the question.*

KITTY. I don't know . . . not really.

BEA. A crisis can be a great opportunity.

KITTY. I'm sure . . .

BEA. You've not found that?

KITTY. No.

> Well yes . . .

> BEA *waits for* KITTY *to say more.*

> But no. I did try . . .

> Well not try, but . . .

> BEA*'s head tilts to one side.*

> No, it's nothing. I had a thing I . . . I wanted to ask my dad . . . it was an important thing, but . . .

BEA. But . . . ?

KITTY (*tries to make light*). Well he's just been in for another awful op. His carotid artery got furred up and they had to . . . well anyway, it was really risky. Afterwards, he was in ICU. I went in, and . . . he was sort of awake – half-watching TV . . . some game show . . .

> KITTY*'s in the moment now.*

> And I took his hand . . . all the tubes in it, and I thought:

> I need to ask him this . . . I mean, he owes me this . . .

> And he turned to me . . . this man who'd lost another of his nine lives, and he said:

> 'They told me I could have a sandwich later. I hope it's not brown bread. That would really ruin my evening.'

> KITTY *shakes her head in disbelief at the bathos of the moment.* BEA *waits, but there's no more.*

BEA. So . . . you didn't ask?

KITTY. Well what do you think?!

BEA (*sighs*). Would you really like to know what I think, Kitty?

A beat before KITTY *manages to answer.*

KITTY. Sure.

BEA. I think you ran away.

KITTY. I've been meaning to get more exercise.

BEA. You can't run for ever.

KITTY. Oh, I don't know.

A stand-off between the women.

BEA. I'm sorry for you, Kitty. You're a time bomb.

KITTY. No I'm not. I'm happy.

The TV laughtrack kicks in. JOHNNY *hurries in with a bowl of snacks, pushes onto the sofa with* MILES. *The TV sound continues, muted. The men laugh along.*

KITTY *takes in* BEA*'s kitchen.*

(*About to leave.*) Well it really looks great, Bea. It's very relaxing. Very light – uncluttered.

BEA. That's the eau-de-Nil.

BEA *lets the eau-de-Nil wash over her.*

The downstairs loo still doesn't flush properly, but . . . You can't have everything.

BEA *smiles, radiant with acceptance. She goes off,* KITTY *watching after her until she sees:*

CARL *holding his balloon, in a separate but connected space. He lets go of the string, watches it float away up into the sky. He turns and looks at* KITTY, *shrugs. Everything's as it should be. But the moment is broken as:*

The Will and Grace *theme tune erupts.*

JOHNNY *and* MILES (*calling out*). Kitty!!!

CARL *laughs. Some acknowledgement between them before he goes off, leaving her to it.*

KITTY *enters the space with* JOHNNY *and* MILES, *absorbs the sight of the men, both transfixed by the screen. They budge apart on the sofa to make room for her. She hesitates, but then moves to settle in between them.* JOHNNY *takes her hand, smiles.* MILES *rests his head against her, easy, relaxed. They all watch the show for a few seconds, then laugh out loud together at the same so-so joke.* KITTY *perhaps less engaged than the men.*

The TV flickers on, a ragged hum of barely audible dialogue, followed by bursts of canned laughter, but JOHNNY*'s already starting to fall asleep. He finally lets go, slumps slightly. Now* MILES*' head tilts back, his eyes starting to close.*

Another burst of laughter, and KITTY *half-laughs to herself. She's relaxing a little now, the shadows from the screen flickering over her face as the light around her fades, throwing her features into relief.*

And the laughtrack goes on, defiantly cheerful, although KITTY *isn't laughing any more. And the TV light plays – oddly intense – over her perfectly inscrutable face.*

Blackout.

The End.